BEC Vant
Testbuilder

Jake Allsop
Tricia Aspinall

◆

MACMILLAN

Macmillan Education
Between Towns Road, Oxford OX4 3PP
A division of Macmillan Publishers Limited
Companies and representatives throughout the world

ISBN 1 405 018348

First published 2004

Original design by Xen Media Ltd
Page layout by eMC Design, www.emcdesign.org.uk
Cover design by Xen Media Ltd

The authors would like to thank Sarah Curtis and Frances Cook for
their help.

The authors and publishers would like to thank the following for
permission to reproduce their material:
Business in East Anglia for extract from 'Norwich Airport:
Refurbishing the terminal' from *Business in East Anglia,*
January/February 1999; **Business Weekly** for extracts from 'So you
want to start a business?' by Gordon Round from *Business Weekly,*
23.04.98; **Executary International** for extract from 'Talk to a
machine' from *Executary International* magazine, Spring 1999;
Haymarket Business Publications Limited for extracts from 'First
class coach' by Miranda Kennett from *Management Today* magazine,
March 2002; **Institute of Directors** for extracts from 'South Africa
Cape of hope' by Lesley Shutte from *Director,* March 2002; 'Talking
shop' by Sophie Chalmers, 'Letter: Searching Questions' by Nikki
Pilkington and 'What's in a name?' by Maureen Moody' all from
Director, December 1998; **Peebles Media** for extracts from 'Beating
the bullies' from *O.S* magazine, Spring 1998; **Philip Allan Updates**
for extracts from 'Finance and the service sector' from *Business
Review* Vol. 8 No.3, February 2002.

Although we have tried to trace and contact copyright holders before
publication, in some cases this has not been possible. If contacted,
we will be pleased to rectify any errors or omissions at the earliest
opportunity.

Printed and bound in Great Britain
by Scotprint

2008 2007 2006 2005
10 9 8 7 6 5 4 3 2

CONTENTS

Introduction   4

INTRODUCTION

The BEC Vantage Testbuilder provides students with the information and practice they need to pass BEC Vantage. It offers teachers and students an encouraging and accessible way to prepare for the exam and may be used as part of a business English course or as a self-access programme for students preparing for the exam on their own. There are four complete practice tests that reflect the content and level of the actual examination. All the tests are of a similar standard and include the themes, topics and vocabulary specified in the BEC Vantage Syllabus. They are accompanied by an expanded answer key and further practice and guidance sections.

Expanded Key

The main purpose of the expanded key is to promote confidence and understanding of the demands of the exam. It gives students and teachers information about why a particular answer is correct and, when appropriate, there are explanations as to why other options or possible answers are incorrect.

Further Practice and Guidance

Each part of the test is accompanied by one or more further practice and guidance sections. The aim of these sections is to give students more information about how to tackle the particular item types in that part of the test. There are also graduated exercises to enable them to improve their test technique as well as their language skills.

The BEC examination covers the four language skills of reading, writing, listening and speaking.

Reading (1 hour)

This test is in five parts. There are 45 questions worth one mark each.

Part One

This is a matching task based on four short texts or one longer text divided into four sections (250–350 words in total). The texts are taken from newspapers, magazines and catalogues. The task is to match seven statements to the relevant text. This part of the test focuses on your ability to identify specific details in the texts. See page 8 for further practice and guidance.

Part Two

This is a matching task consisting of a single text (450–550 words in total) such as an article or a report that has had six sentences removed from it, and a set of seven sentences. The task is to choose one of the set of seven sentences to fit into each gap. The first one is done as an example so you only have to complete five gaps. This part tests your understanding of text structure as well as general comprehension of the text as a whole. See pages 38 and 94 for further practice and guidance.

Part Three

This task is a single text (450–550 words) with six four-option multiple choice questions. The text may be a newspaper article or some business literature including company information and management topics. This part tests your ability to understand the text as a whole and to elicit specific information. See pages 14 and 68 for further practice and guidance.

Part Four

This is a single text (200–300 words) with sixteen gaps. The first one is done as an example. The task is to select the correct answer from a choice of four options. This part tests your vocabulary and understanding of structure. See page 44 for further practice and guidance.

Part Five

This is a proof reading task. The task is to identify words that have been introduced incorrectly into a text. The text (150–200 words) could be a letter, an advertisement or other similar material. See pages 73 and 101 for further practice and guidance.

Writing (45 minutes)

The writing test is in two parts. There are a total of ten possible marks for the first part and a total of twenty possible marks for the second part.

Part One

This task is to produce an internal company communication such as a note, a memo or an email (40–50 words). The information explains the role you are given and the person you are writing to. You are also given some information that must be included in the message.

This part tests your ability to briefly give instructions, explain a development, ask for comments or information or agree to a request. See pages 20 and 75 for further practice and guidance.

Part Two

This task is to produce a piece of business correspondence, a short report or a proposal (120–140 words). The information you are given includes an explanation of the task and one or two texts. These texts are sometimes visual or graphic material with handwritten notes on them. This part tests your ability to explain, apologize, reassure, complain, describe, summarize, recommend or persuade. See pages 49 and 104 for further practice and guidance.

Listening (40 minutes)

The listening test consists of recorded extracts and a written question paper. In the exam, the instructions are on the recording and on the question paper. The test is in three parts and lasts about 30 minutes. In the exam, each section is heard twice and there is an extra ten minutes to transfer the answers on to a special answer sheet. There are 30 questions worth one mark each.

Part One

In this part, there are three conversations or messages and a gapped text for each one. There are four gaps in each text. The texts are forms, invoices and message pads, etc. This part tests your ability to listen for factual information and convert it into a suitable answer to complete the gap. See pages 25 and 110 for further practice and guidance.

Part Two

This part is divided into two sections. You will hear five short monologues in each section and the task is to match each monologue to one of eight options. There is a theme or topic linking each set of options. This part tests your global listening skills and your ability to understand the main idea or gist of the monologues. See pages 53 and 110 for further practice and guidance.

Part Three

There is a longer text in this part of about four minutes. This is an interview, discussion, presentation or report. There are eight three-option multiple choice questions that test your general understanding of ideas and opinions expressed in the recording. See pages 83 and 110 for further practice and guidance.

Speaking (14 minutes)

The speaking test is taken either in pairs or, occasionally, with three candidates. There are two examiners. One of them (the interlocutor) will speak to you and lead you through the tasks. The other examiner just listens. Both examiners are involved in the marking process.
The test is in three parts.

Part One

This part lasts about three minutes. The interlocutor will speak to each of you in turn and ask you general questions about your life, your work or your studies. You are being tested on your ability to talk briefly about yourself and to show you are able to agree, disagree or express preferences. You won't usually be asked exactly the same questions as your partner. See page 30 for further practice and guidance.

Part Two

In this part of the test, you will be asked to give a mini-presentation on a business topic. You and your partner are each given a choice of three topics and you have one minute to prepare your presentation. You are expected to talk for about one minute. When you have finished your presentation, your partner is invited to ask you a question about it. This part tests your ability to speak for an extended period. See page 59 for further practice and guidance.

Part Three

In Part Three, you and your partner are given a topic to discuss for about three minutes. The interlocutor will then ask further questions related to the topic. This part tests your ability to hold a conversation, express opinions, compare and contrast and acknowledge your partner's contributions. You are not expected to reach a joint conclusion and it is acceptable for you both to disagree as long as this is expressed clearly. See pages 88 and 115 for further practice and guidance.

TEST ONE

READING 1 hour

PART ONE

Questions 1–7

- *Look at the statements below and the job advertisements on the opposite page.*

- *Which job advertisement (**A, B, C** or **D**) does each statement 1–7 refer to?*

- *For each statement 1–7, mark one letter (**A, B, C** or **D**).*

- *You will need to use some of these letters more than once.*

Example:

    0   You will need to know a foreign language for this job.

---

1   Your letter of application should not be typed.

2   You must have a science degree for this job.

3   If you are interested in this job, send for an application form.

4   The advertiser wants to know how much you earn in your present job.

5   This is a managerial position.

6   To stay in this job, you need to renew your contract annually.

7   You could get this job without having a degree or diploma.

Before you check your answers, go to pages 8–9.

A

Lecturers in Tourism, Business Management or Media Studies required for the Rosas Excellence Institute. The posts are on the basis of a one-year contract renewable. Candidates need a degree or diploma in a relevant subject and five years' teaching experience. Send CV with covering handwritten letter and details of current salary.

B

Automotive Engineer to take charge of busy Vehicle Maintenance Workshop. The job involves working as part of the management team, and in particular organizing and supervising work schedules and assisting with staff training. A higher qualification in mechanical engineering and previous experience of heavy goods vehicles essential. Send career details with photograph and three professional references.

C

Medical Representative to sell pharmaceutical products to doctors and pharmacies. You need to have a degree in a relevant subject, preferably in biology or chemistry, experience in sales/marketing, and an ability to get on with people. The job offers an excellent salary, benefits and career opportunities. Applications should include CV and mention of expected salary.

D

Junior Officer (Accounts) to help with overseas customer accounts. The successful applicant will be bilingual (in English and Spanish), and will have at least three years' relevant experience. We offer a competitive salary, holiday allowance, bonus scheme and free medical insurance. For further details and an application form, phone or write to Personnel Officer Provenza SA.

EXAM INFORMATION

Part One of the reading test is a matching task and consists of four short texts on a related theme (or sometimes a single text divided into four sections). The texts may include:

- product descriptions
- advertisements for goods or services
- job advertisements
- information notices
- warning notices
- short product reviews.

You are given seven statements and you have to say to which of the four texts each statement refers.

A DETAILED STUDY

The secret of success in this test is careful reading and attention to detail. The same information may occur in more than one text, so you have to look carefully to see which information matches the statement. For example, four business cards might have the following details:

Card A	name	job title	office tel	home tel	mobile	email
Card B	name	job title	office tel	–	–	email
Card C	name	–	office tel	home tel	–	–
Card D	name	job title	–	home tel	mobile	–

If the statement refers to the card that has a job title, mobile number and email, you can see that only Card A has all three.

1   Read the information about four shops on page 9, and then answer the questions. More than one shop may fit the description. Which shop (or shops) will you visit if:

1   you want some fresh vegetables and you want to pay by credit card?

2   Wednesday is the only day you are free to do your shopping?

3   you need some tinned tomatoes and just have a credit card?

4   you like to shop early in the morning for fresh fruit and vegetables?

5   you can't get to the shop till the evening and you want fresh fruit?

Shop A
Opening times: 06.00–15.00, Mon–Sat
Sells: fresh fruit and vegetables
Accepts: cash only

Shop B
Opening times: 08.00–22.00, 7 days a week
Sells: frozen goods, dry and tinned (canned) goods
Accepts: cash or cheque, credit cards

Shop C
Opening times: 08.00–17.00, Mon–Sat
(closed all day Wed)
Sells: dry and tinned (canned) goods
Accepts: cash or cheque

Shop D
Opening times: 10.00–22.00, Mon, Wed, Fri only
Sells: fresh fruit and vegetables, frozen goods, dry and tinned (canned) goods
Accepts: cash or cheque, credit cards

2   Now look at the four job advertisements on page 7. Underline all references to:

   1   qualifications

   2   experience

   3   salary

   4   other terms (benefits) of contract

   5   method of application

Now check your answers and then look back at your answers to Part One of the reading test.

PART TWO

Questions 8–12

- *Read the article below about starting your own business.*

- *Choose the best sentence from the opposite page to fill each of the gaps.*

- *For each gap 8–12, mark one letter (A–G).*

- *Do not use any letter more than once.*

- *There is an example at the beginning (0).*

STARTING YOUR OWN BUSINESS

The first two things to do if you are starting your own business are to find an accountant and talk to your bank manager. Your accountant will help you to draw up a business plan to show what borrowings you need from your bank. **(0)** ....*G*.... .

While you are engaged in these consultations, it is a good idea to find out whether you are entitled to any government subsidies or similar financial help. **(8)** .... Check too whether training grants are available for yourself or people you employ.

Once you have completed these preliminary tasks, there are a number of specific things you then need to do. Doing them in the right way and at the right time can save you a lot of money, so make sure you know what to do.

Perhaps the most important is to tell the Inland Revenue that you have left your job and have started your own business. **(9)** .... The Inland Revenue will also need to amend their records to show that you are now self-employed. Next, you should think about registering for Value Added Tax (VAT). Generally, if your sales exceed a certain amount you have to charge VAT on them. **(10)** ....

Consider the consequences of employing people in your business. As soon as you start to take on employees, you will need to establish proper procedures. These include drawing up proper contracts of employment. You will also need to get in touch with your local tax office to register your employees.

Lastly, as part of becoming an employer of others, you must become familiar with a number of legal issues. Once you have more than a minimum number of people on your payroll, you will need to comply with Health and Safety requirements. **(11)** .... One issue that you should think about once your business expands and your staff grow in numbers is equal opportunity. In particular, you should consider drawing up a company policy on equal opportunity. **(12)** ....

If you need more information on legal or other matters relating to employment, contact your local Chamber of Commerce, which will either be able to help you, or will put you in touch with organizations who can.

Example:

A   It is a good idea, when considering this issue, to ask your local Fire Authority to check your work premises in order to ensure that they comply with current fire regulations.

B   Even if your sales are under that figure, it may be worthwhile registering voluntarily because you could recover what you have been charged on your business purchases.

C   If you are new to this, talk to your local Chamber of Commerce about placing suitable advertisements in the local press.

D   For example, you might be in a less prosperous region where grants are made to encourage the start-up of small businesses.

E   You may be due a repayment of income tax deducted while you were in employment, so do this as soon as possible.

F   If this includes a commitment to employ disabled people, you will need to ensure that your premises are equipped to accommodate them, for example with ramps for wheelchairs, special provision of toilets, and so on.

G   Once this is done, your bank manager will need to review the plan and discuss any overdraft facility you might need.

PART THREE

Questions 13–18

- Read the article below about leadership and the questions on the opposite page.

- For each question **13–18**, mark one letter (**A, B, C** or **D**) for the answer you choose.

FIRST TIME LEADER

Taking on a leadership role for the first time is tough. There is always pressure on you to do the right things, and to be seen to be doing them. But, unless there's
5 something that needs sorting out urgently, your first few months in the role will be better spent in understanding the people and the situation. One easy mistake to make is to think that you, as leader, the top
10 person with the top salary, have the sole responsibility and the know-how to solve every single problem yourself. And you can be sure that others will encourage you to think that way, since it takes the pressure
15 off them, and it satisfies their natural urge to leave the solving of problems to others. Instead try using existing resources to identify the current position and the ways to change it for the better.
20   Start by consulting widely, beginning with the people who now report to you direct, as these are most likely to be the people with the expertise and experience to tackle some of the problems that are
25 identified. A series of one-to-one meetings, though time-consuming, will be worthwhile, especially if they are structured to provide you with the information you need to make decisions later on. Two useful
30 questions are: 'What do you see as the biggest problem facing the department now?' and 'What one change would make the most difference to our success?' From their answers you can build up a picture of
35 your people, as well as of the issues. Some will consider the needs of the department as a whole, while others may just concentrate on their own particular concerns. You will also have had personal
40 contact with each person and can judge who you will work well with in the future.
     Overlap in their responses is a useful pointer to the priorities needing your

attention. If there is no duplication in
45 problems or solutions, it means that you have inherited a disunited group which will need some team-building and restructuring. If no clear picture emerges, it means that your people are part of the problem: you
50 will need to make them aware of this.
     At the same time, consult with customers. Be open to criticizm and to praise. Compare the views of your department with this external viewpoint
55 and see where the biggest gaps are. This will help to identify areas for action.
     While you are data-gathering, have a look at the figures. Apply different measures from the standard ones. You
60 probably lack knowledge about which company products are profitable, and you recognize that staff costs are a key factor. So, ask for an analysis of profitability per employee. There will be some grumbling
65 that the new figures involve extra work, but the analysis will reveal how many and what kind of staff your company really needs.
     Finally, a key issue for you as a new leader is to establish priorities. If you have
70 done your research well, you will have identified a number of areas for action. Bring your senior team together and tell them about your research findings, both the problems and the suggested solutions.
75 Together, plot the solutions on a big graph, with one axis relating to the amount of difference the action would make; and the other axis to the ease of implementation. This will prompt useful discussion on the
80 issues and the means of resolving them. In selecting priorities, you might well gain volunteers to tackle some of the tasks. Agree actions, assign responsibilities and establish dates for completion and progress
85 reviews.

13   Employees encourage their boss to believe that he or she should solve all the problems, because they

   A   really don't want to have to solve the problems themselves.

   B   believe that the boss is paid to solve problems.

   C   know that the boss has a lot more information about the issues than they do.

   D   feel that they shouldn't have to solve problems created by other people.

14   How should you structure your first meetings according to the writer?

   A   Explain to each member of staff the problems facing his or her department.

   B   See people individually and ask each one the same questions.

   C   Ask each member of staff to help in setting priorities for action.

   D   Bring everyone into the discussion to get an agreed plan of action.

15   Getting the same answers from different people during your research tells you that

   A   the people who are under you clearly do not work well together.

   B   a lot of your department's problems are caused by the people themselves.

   C   you have identified the most urgent issues needing your attention.

   D   your department is working well despite a number of problems.

16   It is useful to talk to customers about the performance of your department because

   A   they are likely to be more honest and open than your own staff.

   B   it makes your customers feel that their opinions are important to you.

   C   it gives you an opportunity to criticize or praise them.

   D   you can evaluate what they say against what your own staff told you.

17   What might you learn from the kind of financial analysis that the writer recommends?

   A   that you need to employ fewer people, or people with different skills

   B   that you can increase profitability by using different measures

   C   that this kind of financial analysis involves a lot of extra work

   D   that financial data must be combined with other information to give a full picture

18   According to the writer, using a graph as part of the meeting with senior staff is a good way to

   A   set deadlines for completing the work and reporting back.

   B   give feedback to your staff on the results of your research.

   C   get your staff talking about the issues and what to do about them.

   D   show which members of staff should tackle the various problems.

Before you check your answers, go to pages 14–15.

EXAM INFORMATION

Part Three of the reading test has a text of 450–550 words followed by six four-option multiple choice items. For Questions 13–18, you have to choose the option which best matches the information in the text. This part of the test is designed to see how carefully you read the text, and how well you are able to match the correct option to the relevant information in the text.

The texts are all on business-related topics and deal with such issues as:

- economics and finance
- trade and industry
- starting up or running a business
- management
- careers
- working conditions
- working practices
- office technology.

A DETAILED STUDY

1 Read the text and answer these general questions.

  1 Will the employees talk mainly about their department's problems or about their own problems?

  2 What do you learn if you get similar information and views from several employees?

  3 What do you learn if each employee gives you a different picture?

  4 What does it mean if you really learn very little from your employees?

  5 Apart from interviewing staff, what other sources of information does the writer suggest for the leader?

2 The questions below will help you understand the text better and make sure you choose the correct options for questions 13–18.

  1 What does the phrase *since it takes the pressure off them* mean? (lines 14–15)

  2 What does the expression *one-to-one* mean? (line 25)

  3 Who or what does the word *their* refer to in line 42? Explain the phrase *overlap in their responses is a useful pointer* (lines 42–43).

  4 What do the words *the biggest gaps* refer to? (line 55)

  5 What will *an analysis of profitability per employee* tell you? (lines 63–64)

  6 What does *this* refer to in line 79? Explain the phrase *This will prompt useful discussion …* (line 79).

3   This exercise will help you become more familiar with the text and practise some useful expressions. Underline the following phrases in the text and explain the meaning of the words in italics.

   1   something that needs *sorting out* urgently (line 5)

   2   you have *the sole responsibility* (lines 10–11)

   3   the *know-how* to solve every single problem (line 11)

   4   *their natural urge* to leave the solving of problems to others (lines 15–16)

   5   *try using* existing resources (line 17)

   6   identify *the current position* (line 18)

   7   *tackle* some of the problems (line 24)

   8   *time-consuming* (line 26)

   9   *build up a picture* (line 34)

   10   others may just concentrate on *their own particular concerns* (lines 37–39)

   11   you will need to *make them aware* of this (line 50)

   12   see where *the biggest gaps* are (line 55)

   13   Apply different measures from *the standard ones* (lines 58–59)

   14   *establish priorities* (line 69)

   15   *the ease of implementation* (line 78)

Now check your answers and then look back at your answers to Part Three of the reading test.

PART FOUR

Questions 19–33

- *Read the article below about claiming business travel expenses.*

- *Choose the best word to fill each gap from **A, B, C** or **D** on the opposite page.*

- *For each question **19–33**, mark one letter (**A, B, C** or **D**).*

- *There is an example at the beginning (**0**).*

BUSINESS TRAVEL EXPENSES

Britain's business travellers need to work as many as 3.5 million extra days every year to **(0)** .....B..... the cost of unaccounted-for travel expenses, according to Visa International. Business travellers from six European countries **(19)** .... that they were left out of pocket by nearly £23 per month through forgetting to **(20)** .... back business travel expenditure, or losing expense **(21)** .... Visa **(22)** .... interviews with European business travellers in order to ascertain their **(23)** .... towards travel expenditure and expense reporting. The research **(24)** .... that executives find it easier to **(25)** .... their expenses if they use a company payment card for most of their expenditure. The survey found that many British business travellers have to fund their **(26)** .... completely out of their own pockets and wait to be **(27)** .... by their company. Around half said that they were not given cash prior to going away on business, and over 80% said that they had to **(28)** .... on using their personal credit cards.

In contrast, Spanish and Italian companies generally **(29)** .... their executives with cash. Approximately two thirds of business travellers from these countries said their company gave them cash in **(30)** .... Getting your money back is further **(31)** .... by the fact that almost 20% of European companies refuse to give a refund to employees who cannot produce valid evidence of expenditure.

Companies are losing out too. The survey shows that British business travellers **(32)** .... 7.8 million working days every year filling out their expense forms! But a solution is in sight. The present situation requires the business traveller to take cash to pay for incidental expenses. However, leading card providers are developing 'plastic cash', a card which can be used like a debit card. In this way, the **(33)** .... of using cash can be avoided.

Example:

0   **A** accept   **B** cover   **C** solve   **D** deduct

0	A	B	C	D
	▭	▬	▭	▭

19 **A** assessed   **B** valued   **C** estimated   **D** analyzed

20 **A** claim   **B** ask   **C** demand   **D** require

21 **A** invoices   **B** bills   **C** tickets   **D** receipts

22 **A** conducted   **B** produced   **C** led   **D** caused

23 **A** opinion   **B** behaviour   **C** conduct   **D** attitude

24 **A** exposed   **B** displayed   **C** revealed   **D** uncovered

25 **A** run   **B** manage   **C** control   **D** adopt

26 **A** trips   **B** tours   **C** voyages   **D** excursions

27 **A** returned   **B** rewarded   **C** recompensed   **D** reimbursed

28 **A** count   **B** call   **C** decide   **D** rely

29 **A** supply   **B** equip   **C** involve   **D** treat

30 **A** advance   **B** case   **C** settlement   **D** arrears

31 **A** prevented   **B** hindered   **C** interrupted   **D** obtained

32 **A** pass   **B** bring   **C** spend   **D** use

33 **A** embarrassment   **B** discomfort   **C** inconvenience   **D** disturbance

PART FIVE

Questions 34–45

- Read the article below about answering machines.

- In most of the lines **34–45**, there is one extra word. It is either grammatically incorrect or does not fit in with the sense of the text. Some lines, however, are correct.

- If a line is correct, write **CORRECT**.

- If there is an extra word in the line, write **the extra word** in CAPITAL LETTERS.

- The exercise begins with two examples, **(0)** and **(00)**.

Examples

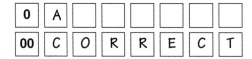

| 0 | A | | | | | |
| 00 | C | O | R | R | E | C | T |

ANSWERING MACHINES

0	We all rely on answering machines and voice mail. Yet a research shows that
00	they are among the most hated things in business life. What's worse, you can
34	easily upset callers with a bad message. Here it is how to improve your message.
35	First, state your name or company. It is frustrating enough not to have speak to
36	someone without wondering if you have even so reached the right person. Ask
37	callers to leave their name, reason for calling and phone number. Thirdly, if you
38	leave out an alternative number, say it slowly. It's also a good idea to let people
39	know when you will pick up your messages. Next, make sure of the bleep sounds
40	immediately after the outgoing message. It is irritating for callers to have to start
41	their message all over there again because the bleep interrupted them. Researchers
42	say that 7 out of 10 callers do not leave messages, so far it may be better to get a
43	phone answering service to handle your calls. In the end, it will cost you too much
44	less to pay an agency to handle your callers than to lose a client but who is unable
45	to get through to you.

WRITING 45 minutes

PART ONE

- *Your office printer has broken down and you decide to replace it.*

- *Write an **email** to the Head of Purchasing:*

    - *describing the reason for not repairing the old one*

    - *explaining what you need from a new one (e.g. colour, paper size)*

    - *suggesting where to buy a new one.*

- ***Write 40–50 words.***

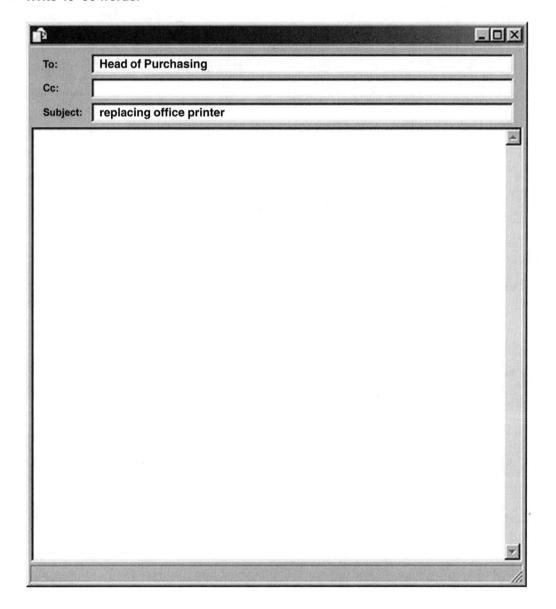

To:	Head of Purchasing
Cc:	
Subject:	replacing office printer

Before you write your email, go to pages 20–21.

EXAM INFORMATION

In Part One of the writing test, you have to produce a communication of 40–50 words
from one person to another in the form of:

- a memo
- an email
- a short note.

The instructions provide a context and tell you who the communication is for as well as listing the
information which must be included in your answer.

The topics are all on business-related matters such as:

- office procedures
- purchasing
- a meeting, conference or exhibition
- travel arrangements
- training
- introducing new systems, e.g. IT
- contracts and deals.

You are usually asked to do three or four things. These may be:

A   giving or confirming information

B   requesting permission

C   explaining what has happened or will happen

D   apologizing

E   making suggestions

F   issuing or accepting/declining an invitation

G   expressing thanks

H   offering or asking for help

I   proposing or accepting a deal

A DETAILED STUDY

1   Look at the following phrases and match them to one of the categories (A–I) above.

    1   Ms Graziani is very happy to meet you for dinner on Friday.

    2   ... we have installed an improved sprinkler system ...

    3   If there is any way we can be of assistance to you, please ask.

    4   ... here are the invoice numbers you asked for: 545, 547 and 560.

    5   ... apparently it was a power surge that caused our computers to crash.

    6   Subject to your agreement to increase our share to 35%, we are happy to become distributors of
your products.

7   ... it might be a good idea to update all our sales literature ...

8   If you find the franchise arrangements acceptable, I will draw up a contract immediately.

9   I wonder if I might be allowed to reorganize the office filing system.

10   ... we would like you to join us for cocktails after the AGM ....

11   I want everyone to make the new trainees feel at home.

12   The Principal wishes to express his gratitude for all your hard work.

2   Read the answer which a student wrote to the question in Part One. Then answer the questions below.

> There's no point in repairing the old printer because it will cost more to repair our old printer than to by a new one. Another thing: what we need is really good printer that will product better colour quality. There's a company called Printers-R-Us that do some good deals right now. I suggest to give them a bell.

[58 words]

1   Does the email follow the instructions?

2   Find two spelling mistakes in the email.

3   Find three grammatical mistakes in the email.

4   The student has used informal expressions in two places in the email which are not appropriate. Find the expressions. Can you make them more appropriate?

5   The student has written eight words too many. Can you reduce the number of words?

Now write your own answer to Part One of the writing test. Remember to check for grammar and spelling mistakes.

PART TWO

- *A branch of your company is moving to another town. The company Chairman has asked you to investigate and recommend a removals company.*

- *Look at the two advertisements below, on which you have already made some handwritten notes.*

- *Then, using **all** your handwritten notes, write your **proposal** for the Chairman.*

- ***Write 120–140 words.***

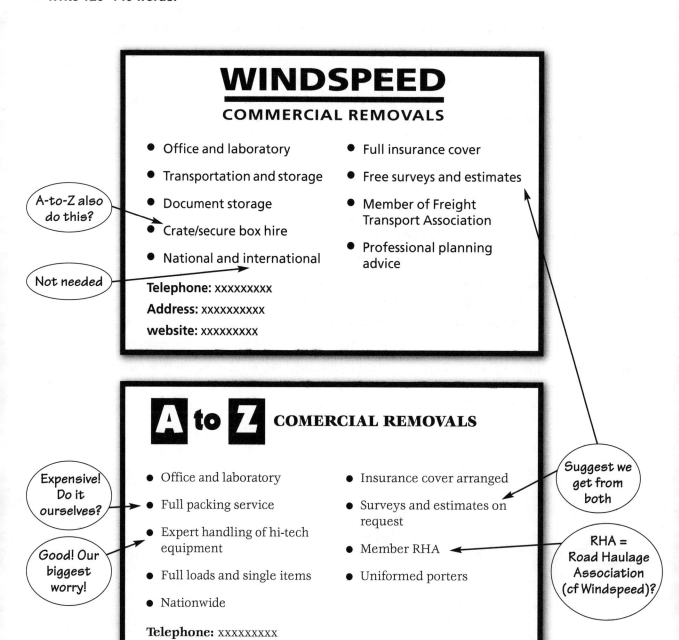

LISTENING approx. 40 minutes

PART ONE
Questions 1–12

Before you answer questions 1–12, go to page 25.

- *You will hear three telephone conversations or messages.*

- *Write **one or two words or a number** in the numbered spaces on the notes or forms below.*

Conversation One
(Questions 1–4)

- *Look at the form below.*

- *You will hear a woman asking questions about a training course.*

Personnel Department   **Training Section**

Personnel Officer: David Jones

Course: Health and Safety

Date: 10/4/04

Course code: (1) ....

(2) Course ....: John Briggs

Seminar room: (3) ....

Please wear clothes* suitable for activities which may involve contact with the floor and use of **(4)** .... equipment.

* e.g. track-suits

Conversation Two

(Questions 5–8)

- *Look at the note below.*

- *You will hear a man leaving a message on a telephone answering service.*

Message received for: Paul Ryman

From: Mark Nolan (Winston House)

Wants to know how many delegates for the plenary sessions. Has reserved three rooms for you.

Choice is between the **(5)** .... (will hold up to 100) or the

Garden Room in the **(6)** .... The two other rooms are on the second floor of the main

hotel and there is **(7)** .... for wheelchair users.

As soon as he has some idea of how many are coming by car he will **(8)** ....

You can call him on extension 457.

Conversation Three

(Questions 9–12)

- *Look at the form below.*

- *You will hear a man telephoning about an incorrect order.*

Order Amendment Form

Our Ref: AZ56W/402

(9) ....: 1005016900

Order Number: W36936Q **(10)** ....

Code	Product	Qty	Price	Post & packing	Total
6694	Parnell Corner Desk	1	£394		
6693	Parnell **(11)**	1	£189	**(12)**	£583

Comment: Customer received incorrect invoice. Please annul original order form.

EXAM INFORMATION

In Part One of the listening test you hear three conversations or messages. For each conversation or message, there is a gapped text with four spaces that you have to fill with one or two words or a number. The gapped texts are either forms, sets of notes, invoices or diary extracts, etc.

The aim of this part of the test is to assess your ability to retrieve factual information. The answers are very specific and must be spelt correctly if the spelling is given during the recording. The gapped text does not repeat the words used in the recording exactly so you need to listen carefully and be prepared to reformulate some of what you hear.

In the exam you will hear each recorded conversation or message twice.

A DETAILED STUDY

1   Read through the gapped texts carefully and decide what sort of answer is expected. For example, in Conversation 1 you should look for the following sorts of words:

   1   a number or a mixture of letters and numbers

   2   a word which goes with 'course' and describes what John Briggs does

   3   a location

   4   a word that describes the type of equipment they will be using

2   Now read Conversations 2 and 3 and do the same thing.

   Conversation 2

   5   ....

   6   ....

   7   ....

   8   ....

   Conversation 3

   9   ....

   10   ....

   11   ....

   12   ....

3   Listen to the recording for Conversation 1 and fill in the gaps. Check your answers. How many of the gaps require more than one word?

4   Compare the tapescript for Conversation 1 on page 141 with your completed text. Underline those parts of the tapescript that relate to answers 1–4.

   Does the order of the recording always follow the order of the text?

Now you are ready to listen to Part One of the listening test and answer questions 1–12.

PART TWO

Questions 13–22

Section One

(Questions 13–17)

- *You will hear five short recordings.*

- *For each recording, decide what the speaker's job is.*

- *Write one letter (**A–H**) next to the number of the recording.*

- *Do not use any letter more than once.*

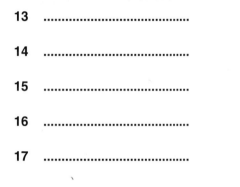

13	....	**A**	Conference Organizer
		B	Personal Assistant
14	....	**C**	Chief Executive
		D	Warehouse Manager
15	....	**E**	Personnel Officer
		F	Accounts Clerk
16	....	**G**	Software Technician
		H	Hotel Receptionist
17	....		

Section Two

(Questions 18–22)

- *You will hear another five recordings.*

- *For each recording, decide what aspects of a colleague each speaker is complaining about.*

- *Write one letter (**A–H**) next to the number of the recording.*

- *Do not use any letter more than once.*

18	....	**A**	poor communicator
		B	unpunctual
19	....	**C**	untidy
		D	unfriendly
20	....	**E**	lazy
		F	disorganized
21	....	**G**	unreliable
		H	bossy
22	....		

PART THREE

Questions 23–30

- *You will hear a conversation between two senior managers discussing how to make their business more successful.*

- *For each question 23–30, mark one letter (**A, B** or **C**) for the correct answer.*

23 Alain thinks the company is in trouble because

    A the workforce is unhappy.

    B there is pressure from overseas.

    C there is insufficient marketing.

24 Lisa thinks the best thing to do is to

    A reduce staffing levels.

    B reduce bonus payments.

    C reduce overtime rates.

25 What do they both agree to do?

    A meet with Union representatives

    B arrange a meeting with the Chief Executive

    C consult with the Board of Directors

26 What does Alain think should be in the strategy document?

    A a research and development programme

    B an economic forecast for the next five years

    C a plan to restructure the company

27 Lisa thinks that most staff will

    A understand the company's position.

    B react badly to any redundancies.

    C agree to the new conditions.

28   Alain thinks that Lisa should

    A   offer to take a redundancy package.

    B   ask for a substantial pay rise.

    C   create a new job for herself.

29   Why is Lisa unhappy with Alain's suggestion?

    A   She doesn't trust him.

    B   She thinks he is joking.

    C   She doesn't understand him.

30   What do they decide to do after their discussion?

    A   go home and think about it

    B   discuss it again after the weekend

    C   write a paper for the Chief Executive

SPEAKING 14 minutes

PART ONE

The interview – about 3 minutes

In Part One of the speaking test, the interlocutor asks questions to each of the candidates in turn. You have to give information about yourself and express personal opinions.

Here are some questions you may be asked:

> What sort of job do you do?
>
> Can you tell me a bit about your work?
>
> What opportunities are there for working abroad?
>
> What is it about your job that you enjoy?
>
> What aspects of your work are you not so keen on?
>
> What qualifications do you need to do a job such as yours?
>
> What skills are important for your sort of work?
>
> What do you see yourself doing in a few years' time?
>
> Do you have any particular ambitions or hopes for the future?

Now go to pages 30–31.

EXAM INFORMATION

The speaking test is taken in pairs (or threes when there is an extra candidate left over). There are two examiners. The interlocutor is the examiner who speaks to you and asks the questions. The other examiner observes and marks you. The interlocutor contributes to the marking process by awarding you one overall mark. You are awarded marks using the following criteria:

- grammar and vocabulary
- discourse management
- pronunciation
- interactive communication.

Part One: The interview

In the first part of the speaking test, the examiner asks you questions about yourself, your work or studies, and other personal matters. This part of the test lasts about three minutes and is designed to test your ability to talk about yourself concisely and to perform certain functions such as agreeing and disagreeing, and expressing personal opinions. You will be asked approximately the same number of questions as your partner, but not necessarily the same questions or in the same order. Listen carefully to the questions you are asked. Avoid giving long, prepared speeches as you may not be answering the question properly.

A DETAILED STUDY

1   Read the following questions and match them to an appropriate answer (A–L). If you can, extend your response, but make sure you only add relevant information.

   1   What sort of job do you do?

   2   Can you tell me a bit about your work?

   3   What opportunities are there for working abroad?

   4   What is it about your job that you enjoy?

   5   What aspects of your work are you not so keen on?

   6   What qualifications do you need to do a job such as yours?

   7   What skills are important for your sort of work?

   8   What do you see yourself doing in a few years' time?

   9   Do you have any particular ambitions or hopes for the future?

   A   Yes. I hope that I will have a more interesting job with a higher salary.

   B   I don't enjoy taking exams very much.

   C   I don't particularly like keying in data.

   D   I'm the marketing manager for a small company.

   E   I spend a lot of time preparing for meetings and dealing with correspondence.

   F   I like the people I work with.

   G   My home town is Novi Sad but I'm working in Belgrade at the moment.

   H   Probably much the same but with more responsibility.

   I   You have to have a degree in engineering.

   J   Lots. We have three factories in France and one in Spain.

   K   Let me see. I'm the eldest of four and the only one working.

   L   You need to be able to communicate well with people.

2   Match the following extended responses to the answers above (A–L).

   1   I find it terribly boring but it has to be done.

   2   We are all about the same age and we support each other a lot.

   3   In fact, I am going to our Madrid factory next week to see how they do things there.

   4   I just get very nervous but I love studying.

   5   And they like you to have done some sort of management course.

   6   I suppose the main part of my job is to make sure everything in the office runs smoothly.

   7   My two brothers and my sister still live at home.

   8   I like my job a lot and I don't really want to do anything different.

   9   It's a food manufacturing company. We make yoghurts and dairy desserts. That sort of thing.

   10   It's not a bad place but I miss my friends and family.

   11   We have a lot of foreign visitors. You need to know how to make them feel comfortable.

   12   What I'm doing now is good experience but it's not particularly challenging.

3   In exercises 1 and 2 there were answers and extended responses that did not fit any of the questions. Which ones were they?

Exercise 1 (answers)

1 ....   **2** ....   **3** ....

Exercise 2 (extended responses)

1 ....   **2** ....   **3** ....

4   Match the answers and extended responses you found in exercise 3 to the questions below.

   1   So, Camille, what's it like being a student?

         (answer) ....

         (extended response) ....

   2   Where do you come from originally, Sasha?

         (answer) ....

         (extended response) ....

   3   Tell me a bit about yourself, Benoit.

         (answer) ....

         (extended response) ....

Now look again at the sample questions in Part One of the speaking test.

PART TWO

Mini-presentation – about 6 minutes

In this part of the test, you are asked to give a short talk on a business topic. You have to choose one of the topics from the three below and then talk for about one minute. You have one minute to prepare your ideas.

A: WHAT IS IMPORTANT WHEN ...?

Interviewing someone for a job

- Deciding what qualifications are needed
- Deciding what questions to ask

B: WHAT IS IMPORTANT WHEN ...?

Arranging a meeting

- Deciding who needs to be there
- Sending out important papers

C: WHAT IS IMPORTANT WHEN ...?

Giving a presentation

- Preparing materials carefully
- Keeping calm

When you have given your presentation, your partner will ask you a question about what you have said. Here are some questions they may ask you:

What did you mean when you said …?

Can you say a bit more about what you said about …?

A   What is the most important thing you would be looking for?

   Is there a question you would always ask?

   What makes a good interviewer?

B   What is the most important thing to do?

   Is it important to choose the right sort of room?

   How do you remind yourself what to do?

C   Do you sometimes get nervous?

   What sort of presentations have you given?

   Do you dress in a certain way?

PART THREE

Discussion – about 5 minutes

In this part of the test, you are given a discussion topic. You have 30 seconds to look at this prompt card and then about 3 minutes to discuss the topic with your partner. After that the examiner will ask you more questions related to the topic.

*For **two** candidates*

Staff training day: Listening to customers

Your company has received several complaints from customers about how their concerns have been handled.

You have been asked to talk to your staff about how to improve the way they listen and respond to customers.

Discuss the situation together, and decide:

- what aspects of customer care your staff need to be aware of
- how you will monitor their dealings with customers.

---

*For **three** candidates*

Staff training day: Listening to customers

Your company has received several complaints from customers about how their concerns have been handled.

You have been asked to talk to your staff about how to improve the way they listen and respond to customers.

Discuss the situation together, and decide:

- what aspects of customer care your staff need to be aware of
- how you will monitor their dealings with customers
- what feedback and evaluation should take place at a later stage.

The interlocutor will then ask you some follow-up questions. Here are some questions you may be asked:

How important do you think customer care is?

What negative reactions might you get from some staff about this sort of training?

Do you think it's important to feed back to staff? Why?

Do you think customers notice if staff have been trained in this way? What will they notice?

TEST TWO

READING 1 hour

PART ONE

Questions 1–7

- *Look at the statements below and the descriptions of events on the opposite page.*

- *Which event (A, B, C or D) does each statement 1–7 refer to?*

- *For each statement 1–7, mark one letter (A, B, C or D).*

- *You will need to use some of these letters more than once.*

Example:

    0   A good opportunity to meet new people who could be of use to you.

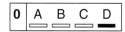

---

1   There is no charge for this event.

2   You will have to share a room if you attend this event.

3   This event will be useful if you have a number of people working under you.

4   If you want to learn how to get on in your career, go to this event.

5   If your job involves documents in foreign languages, this event will interest you.

6   This event is of particular interest to people who work in financial institutions.

7   This is the course for you if you want to learn about organizing events.

A

Personal Assistants. This event is of particular interest to senior secretarial staff working in specialist areas, including banking, accountancy, investment and stocks and shares. Seminar topics include technical report writing, machine translation and interpreter skills. There will also be workshops in specific computer-related areas, including graphics packages and the use of spreadsheets and databases. Please note that the fee covers all seminars, one workshop and all course materials.

B

Business Communications. If you are ambitious, this course is for you! It is designed for PAs and Private Secretaries who want to improve their presentation skills, to gain added confidence through assertiveness training and to learn about the latest developments in office technology. The course also includes a session on further opportunities for professional training. Conference fees include accommodation in twin-bedded rooms*, all meals and transfer to and from the conference centre.
*Single-room supplement available.

C

Senior Secretaries. This event offers an opportunity for Executive Secretaries to keep abreast of developments in their field, to gain an insight into the changes influencing their roles, and above all to demonstrate ways of developing their careers. The key issues to be covered include: dealing with change; managing staff; setting up in-house training programmes; and personal career planning. The cost of the two-day conference includes all course notes, refreshments and lunch.

D

Executive Secretaries. This event provides an opportunity to broaden your business contacts and to gain practical advice from experts in such areas as choosing the best office products, staying abreast of developments in business technology, and planning successful conferences, trade fairs and exhibitions. Experts will also be on hand to advise on effective purchasing practices and ways in which to increase the efficiency of your office. Admission is free, but you are advised to book early as places are limited.

PART TWO

Questions 8–12

- *Read the article below about doing business in Brazil.*

- *Choose the best sentence from the opposite page to fill each of the gaps.*

- *For each gap 8–12, mark one letter (A–G).*

- *Do not use any letter more than once.*

- *There is an example at the beginning, (0).*

BUSINESS PROTOCOL IN BRAZIL

First things first: North Americans should never refer to their country as 'America'. **(0)** ....*G*..... . South Americans, particularly Brazilians, find North Americans arrogant when they refer to back home as 'America'. After all, Brazilians live in America too.

Brazilians take pride in their Portuguese heritage, so to call locals Spanish-Americans would be insulting. On the same note, Brazil's official language is Portuguese, not Spanish. Frequently, the spelling of Portuguese words is exactly the same as Spanish, but the pronunciation differs greatly. **(8)** ....

If your business destination is Rio de Janeiro, land of carnival and the samba, expect a somewhat casual environment. **(9)** .... Bring comfortable semi-casual clothes for business in Rio, and conservative dark suits or dresses for São Paulo. Time is important in São Paulo and lateness is considered rude and unbusinesslike. **(10)** .... If you called a meeting at four, a Rio citizen may interpret gathering time as around four (like maybe four-fifteen or so). Whatever you do, don't be put off or indicate that you were concerned about the late arrival; your South American counterpart won't understand.

Shaking hands and exchanging business cards begins any first business meeting in Brazil. At that time, introductions are made. Formalize your contact's first name by preceding it with *Senhor*, *Senhora* or *Senhorita* (Mr, Mrs or Miss). The surname is not generally used. **(11)** .... In that manner, once you've become friendly with Senhora Astrud, you would be expected to simply call her Astrud.

If you are indicating approval on a business matter, never give the OK sign of a ring formed by the thumb and index finger. **(12)** .... Instead, close the fist and shoot the thumb up. During the business day you will most likely be offered *cafezinho*, a very strong Brazilian coffee. Accept it graciously so as not to offend your host. If you don't like coffee, sip it slowly.

Example:

A   In Rio, on the other hand, your host may not always be so punctual.

B   So, before opening your mouth in this country, learn to speak a few words and avoid committing a cultural offence.

C   This is a very impolite gesture in Brazil and likely to cause great offence.

D   However, when scheduling meetings in São Paulo, you'll find business settings just the opposite: quite formal.

E   Good manners and polite behaviour are highly valued in business dealings in Brazil.

F   Soon after this formality, the title is usually dropped at the request of your host.

G   It is better to say you're from the United States.

Before you check your answers, go to pages 38–39.

EXAM INFORMATION

Part Two of the reading test is a text with gaps where six sentences have been removed. You are given seven sentences to fill six of the gaps (one of the sentences is not needed). You have to match each gap with the sentence that fits in both meaning and structure.

A DETAILED STUDY

The texts in this part always contain a line of thought, where one idea or fact is linked logically to the one before or after it. First, read the text and the sentences in order to understand the line of thought. Look for meaning, but also look out for single words or short phrases such as:

- pronouns, e.g. *it, their*
- demonstratives, e.g. *this, that*
- phrases, e.g. *So ..., On the other hand ..., However ...*
- comparisons, e.g. *better than, prefer (one thing to another).*

Consider how they link one idea to another.

1   This exercise familiarizes you with the main points of the text. Answer the following questions.

    1   Why should people from the USA not call their country *America*?

    2   Why is it insulting to call Brazilians *Spanish-Americans*?

    3   What is a *casual environment*? (paragraph 3)

    4   What should a visitor do if his/her Brazilian contact arrives late for a business meeting?

    5   How does a first business meeting start in Brazil?

    6   What gesture do Brazilians use to signify approval?

    7   What is *cafezinho* and how should a visitor deal with it?

2   What do the words or phrases in italics refer to in the following sentences? (They are all taken from the text.)

    1   North Americans should never refer to *their* country ...

    2   *After all*, Brazilians live in America too.

    3   ..., *so* to call locals Spanish-Americans would be insulting.

    4   *On the same note,* Brazil's official language is Portuguese, not Spanish.

    5   *At that time,* introductions are made.

    6   *Instead,* close the fist ...

    7   Accept *it* graciously ...

3   Now look at items A–G and answer the questions. This exercise helps you to relate the items to their proper place in the text. (Remember, one item does not belong in the text.)

    A   In Rio, *on the other hand,* your host may not always be *so* punctual.
        What comparison is the writer making here?

    B   *So*, before opening your mouth in this country, ...
        Here *So* means *Because of what has just been said* ... What does *So* refer back to?

    C   *This* is a very impolite gesture in Brazil ...
        What does the word *This* refer to?

D   *However,* when scheduling meetings in São Paulo, you'll find business settings
just the opposite: quite formal.
What does *However* mean here? What does *just the opposite* refer to?

E   Good manners and polite behaviour are highly valued in business dealings in Brazil.
Is there a linking device in this sentence?

F   Soon after *this formality,* the title is usually dropped at the request of your host.
What formality is the writer referring to?

G   It is *better* to say you're from the United States.
What does the word *better* refer to?

4   Complete 1–5 with an appropriate phrase or sentence (A–E). Underline the words which link the two
items in each case.

1   It will take us all day to finish this report,

2   Labour costs in this country are very high.

3   Most people use word processors these days,

4   The reps enjoy visiting the Far East on business.

5   Unlike most people, I enjoy writing reports.

A   but a few still prefer to use pen and paper.

B   I just wish they didn't have to be done so quickly.

C   On the other hand, they wouldn't like to live there.

D   so the boss will have to wait till tomorrow for it.

E   That's why the company is relocating to Karachi.

5   When working with texts, you can expand your vocabulary by word building. This means that you can
look up words in your dictionary and find other words related to them, e.g. *satisfy* (verb), *satisfaction*
(noun) and *satisfactory* (adjective).

Complete the following tables. All the words are taken from the text.

Noun	Adjective
1	arrogant
pride	2 ....
lateness	3 ....
4	rude
5	important

Noun	Verb
6	refer
arrival	7 ....
approval	8 ....
9	offer
10	accept
11	interpret
pronunciation	12 ....

Noun	Verb	Adjective
13	differ	14 ....
15	indicate	16 ....
introduction	17	18 ....
19	expect	20 ....
21	offend	22 ....
23	24	insulting

*Now check your answers to these questions and then look back at your answers to Part Two
of the reading test.*

PART THREE

Questions 13—18

- *Read the article below about business names and the questions on the opposite page.*

- *For each question 13–18, mark one letter (A, B, C or D) for the answer you choose.*

SELECTING YOUR BUSINESS NAME

The right business name is important. If you choose the wrong one, you might end up with something that sends all the wrong messages. To be successful, your
5 business name needs to define your identity and say what's special about what you are offering. Think about the market you want to sell into, and why your customer will prefer to buy YOUR product or service rather
10 than someone else's. A good business name is one that tells customers what to expect. For example, Early Learning Centre appeals to parents because it tells them that the toys it sells are educational.

15   Illiterate names have caught on everywhere, that is names that involve deliberately misspelled words. Kwik-Fit, the company that promises to fit car parts speedily, was one of the first in the UK. The
20 name was the brainchild of Kwik-Fit's chief executive, who, as a schoolboy, earned extra pocket money cleaning ovens. He advertised himself as Kookers Kleaned! Some people grumble about these misspellings, arguing,
25 for example, that children will copy them, but even these purists don't hesitate to buy an ice cream from Phun Phlavours! These misspellings work because they catch the eye. The trouble is, as more and more are
30 invented, they lose their impact.

        But unusual names are not always the most effective. Names like Tie Rack or Body Shop which just say what your company is about can work just as well. They are short,
35 and they have an honest no-nonsense ring to them. Sometimes using a personal name can achieve the same effect: Laura Ashley projects a gentle and elegant image that makes the customer feel comfortable about
40 buying that company's products.

        If you are providing a service, decide whether your company name should describe your customer's problem or your unique solution to the problem. For
45 example, a vehicle breakdown service could call itself Panic Breakdowns, which only serves to emphasize the negative state of mind of the customer; or Instant Rescue, which sends out a reassuring message that
50 help is at hand. Which name would you select if you had a burst water pipe: Flood Warning or Peace of Mind?

        Consider too the impact your name will have when people hear it or read it. What
55 effect does it have when spoken over the telephone? Snappy Happy Snaps may describe your photographic agency, but it sounds ridiculous over the phone. When your name appears in Yellow Pages or
60 similar directories, usually amongst a hundred others offering a similar service, you want yours to be the one that catches the eye. One trick is to ensure that the first letter of your name appears early in the
65 alphabet. A business in Finland called itself by the meaningless name Quello, simply because there is no letter Q in Finnish, so Quello was the only entry in the directory under that letter!

70   If you deal with overseas customers, check that your name won't cause you problems. A good translation agency will help you avoid the trap of choosing a name that means something offensive in another
75 language. There is a famous case of a stick deodorant manufactured by an Asian company who had selected a name which meant something really bad in English. The matter was made worse by the instruction
80 printed on it in English, which read 'Push up bottom'.

13 According to the writer, a business name is a good one if it

    A   identifies your market needs.

    B   avoids confusion with other companies.

    C   creates a different kind of image.

    D   persuades people to use your company.

14 What is the writer's attitude to the use of illiterate names?

    A   They have been used so much that people no longer notice them.

    B   They are bad because children will learn wrong spellings.

    C   They are good because people find them amusing.

    D   They fail to describe the service or product accurately.

15 What does the writer like about simple company names?

    A   They accurately describe the product.

    B   They inspire confidence.

    C   They give a personal touch.

    D   They are easy to remember.

16 Which name, Flood Warning or Peace of Mind, would the writer probably prefer?

    A   Flood Warning because it shows the company understands the problem.

    B   Peace of Mind because Flood Warning sounds more serious than a burst pipe.

    C   Peace of Mind because it is designed to comfort the customer.

    D   Flood Warning, because few people know the expression 'peace of mind'.

17 According to the writer, you can help to make your company name stand out by

    A   using an initial letter that gets your name into the front of directories.

    B   making sure the name of your company has an unusual letter in it.

    C   choosing a short name that people can say easily over the phone.

    D   putting your advertisement in several different directories.

18 What advice does the writer give to companies who sell overseas?

    A   Provide a translation of your company name into your customer's language.

    B   Use a good translation agency to translate the product instructions.

    C   Describe your product in simple language that a foreign customer can understand.

    D   Be sure that your company name is not a rude word in another language.

PART FOUR
Questions 19–33

- *Read the article below about promoting Honduran companies.*

- *Choose the best word to fill each gap from **A, B, C** or **D** on the opposite page.*

- *For each question **19–33**, mark one letter (**A, B, C** or **D**).*

- *There is an example at the beginning, (**0**).*

FINANCIAL HELP FOR HONDURAN COMPANIES

A $160 million project to make the 'Made in Honduras' label better known abroad has just been announced in Tegucigalpa. The 'Brandname Fund', as it is called, is a project backed by the Honduran government to (**0**) .....A..... local companies a larger share in world markets. It is the first ever government (**19**) .... of its kind.

A government spokesman announced that the fund would be (**20**) .... in the next few days, and would help Honduran companies to (**21**) .... specific brands.

But business people are doubtful about the scheme's likely (**22**) .... Critics say that not enough money has been put into the fund to make it really (**23**) .... They say that the (**24**) .... is too little to help the many small companies whose limited (**25**) .... prevent them from making a serious impact on international markets.

The Honduran economy was once completely (**26**) .... to foreign investment, but it opened up to foreign companies five or so years ago under sweeping reforms (**27**) .... by the new government. The moves have so far (**28**) .... more than $20 billion worth of foreign investment.

But although certain Honduran (**29**) .... , such as clothing and textiles, bananas and coffee, do quite well, no single Honduran brand has yet (**30**) .... the top rank. The fund is a serious (**31**) .... to change this. The government (**32**) .... , however, that brands selected for promotion abroad should be of international quality and (**33**) .... of making a real impact in the global market.

Example:

    0   **A** give   **B** make   **C** earn   **D** bring

0	A	B	C	D
	▬	▭	▭	▭

19 **A** function   **B** event   **C** advertisement   **D** campaign

20 **A** launched   **B** fired   **C** pronounced   **D** engaged

21 **A** invent   **B** promote   **C** support   **D** develop

22 **A** benefits   **B** assets   **C** profits   **D** dividends

23 **A** definite   **B** certain   **C** effective   **D** capable

24 **A** addition   **B** quantity   **C** amount   **D** size

25 **A** properties   **B** stocks   **C** qualities   **D** resources

26 **A** closed   **B** shut   **C** denied   **D** refused

27 **A** provided   **B** presented   **C** introduced   **D** discovered

28 **A** claimed   **B** caught   **C** persuaded   **D** attracted

29 **A** products   **B** types   **C** makes   **D** names

30 **A** brought   **B** reached   **C** obtained   **D** performed

31 **A** trial   **B** attempt   **C** concern   **D** business

32 **A** defines   **B** reserves   **C** presumes   **D** insists

33 **A** confident   **B** worthy   **C** capable   **D** aware

Before you check your answers, go to pages 44–45.

EXAM INFORMATION

Part Four consists of a text with sixteen gaps. The first one is done for you as an example. You have to choose the word that best fits each gap from fifteen four-option multiple choice items. All the choices will fit grammatically, but only one option fits the meaning. This part of the test is designed to see if you can distinguish between words of similar meaning.

A DETAILED STUDY

1   Answer the following questions to help you with the general meaning of the text.

   1   What is the overall aim of the 'Brandname Fund'?

   2   What experience does the government have of this kind of project?

   3   How do local business people feel about the scheme?

   4   What is the history of foreign investment in Honduran businesses?

   5   What Honduran products do well?

   6   What must be done to make Honduran products acceptable in world markets?

2   To improve and widen your vocabulary, you will need to check dictionary definitions. Match each of the following words to their definitions. All the words are options in the test.

   1   **A** function   **B** event   **C** advertisement   **D** campaign

      1   anything which happens; any memorable incident or occurrence

      2   a solemn service, ceremony or social gathering

      3   an organized series of activities aimed at achieving some goal or object

      4   a public notice designed to inform, change attitudes or persuade to buy

   2   **A** invent   **B** promote   **C** support   **D** develop

      1   create or design something for the first time

      2   bring out the potential in somebody/something, or to cause something to grow

      3   encourage the sales of something through advertising

      4   back up or maintain a loyal interest in somebody/something

   3   **A** benefits   **B** assets   **C** profits   **D** dividends

      1   the share of money due to each individual, usually by way of interest on invested capital

      2   the entire property of all sorts belonging to a merchant or to a trading association

      3   any set of advantages, natural or other

      4   gains resulting from the excess of selling price over first cost

4   **A** properties   **B** stocks   **C** qualities   **D** resources

    1 characteristics or qualities of somebody/something, or things such as buildings which you own

    2 what you have, e.g. money, equipment or staff in order to do a job

    3 the special features that make a thing what it is

    4 units of ownership of a company, consisting of a group of shares; also, a supply of goods, material or equipment for sale

5   **A** products   **B** types   **C** makes   **D** names

    1 examples or models which exemplify the characteristics of a group

    2 the different brands or versions of a manufactured object

    3 that by which a person or thing is known

    4 things which a company manufactures for sale

Now check your answers to these questions and then look back at your answers to Part Four of the reading test.

PART FIVE

Questions 34–45

- *Read the article below about answering machines.*

- *In most of the lines 34–45, there is one extra word. It is either grammatically incorrect or does not fit in with the sense of the text. Some lines, however, are correct.*

- *If a line is correct, write CORRECT.*

- *If there is an extra word in the line, write the extra word in CAPITAL LETTERS.*

- *The exercise begins with two examples, (0) and (00).*

Examples

| 0 | C | O | R | R | E | C | T |

| 00 | B | E | E | N | | | |

WHO NEEDS A HARD COPY?

---

0   Despite advances in data-storage technology and huge hard-disk drives, the

00   volume of paper in the average office has been continued to grow. The reason

34   for this is that computers who have printers attached to them! While the younger

35   generation are comfortable to working on screen, a lot of older people are not

36   happy with a document draft unless they have a printed copy of it. There was

37   used to be a good reason for this. Older computer programs were generally not

38   capable of producing screen previews of what it was to be printed, and you

39   simply had to see a draft copy. Those days are now long gone. Word processing

40   programs today they are capable of showing, on screen, exactly what the output

41   will look like, so many that hard-copy drafts are generally not required for

42   documents. Despite of this, people still want copies 'for the file'. But, in doing

43   so, they miss the point, because the document is already on file! Printing it out is

44   wasteful, because every print cartridges and paper are both very expensive. On

45   the other hand, disk drives are now big enough that they are a much more

         better way of storing data.

WRITING 45 minutes

PART ONE

- *Your company has introduced new Saga accounting software and you think you need training in its use.*

- *Write a **memo** to your line manager:*

  - *saying what you need*

  - *describing a suitable course*

  - *asking for permission to attend.*

- **Write 40–50 words.**

Memo

To: Line Manager

From:

Date: 20th May

Subject: new Saga accounting software

PART TWO

- *You are the manager of a hotel which offers conference facilities. You have received a marked-up copy of your advertisement together with a letter of complaint.*

- *Write a **letter of apology** referring to the customer's four points and either offering an explanation or outlining what action is to be taken in each case.*

- *Write 120–140 words.*

FAIRCHILD'S HOTEL

Hold your next big event by the sea!

- Conferences, sales meetings, functions

- Hi-tech audiovisual facilities[1]

- Social events a speciality

- Comfortable lounges

- Noted for excellent cuisine[2]

- En-suite accommodation

- Off-season discounts[3]

Bookings: 0193 247016.

For more information, visit our website: www.fairfields.co.uk[4]

Contact us by email: fairfields@fairfields.net

---

1 The technical support was not very good.

2 As to your claim about 'excellent cuisine', I must tell you that the food was often cold.

3 We held our conference in February, i.e. off-season, but we seem to have been charged at peak rates.

4 One last point: when we tried to log on to your website, we got a 'page unavailable' message.

Before you write your letter, go to page 49.

EXAM INFORMATION

In Part Two of the writing test, you have to write 120–140 words in the form of business correspondence (letter, fax or email), a short report or a proposal. Typically, you will have information in the form of:

- written texts, e.g. a note, a letter, a memo, an email
- graphics, e.g. a table, a diagram, a pie chart
- printed matter, e.g. an advertisement, an extract from a catalogue.

Often the texts include someone's handwritten comments or instructions. You have to write an appropriate response combining and/or interpreting the information. In business correspondence, you may have to:

- explain
- reassure
- apologize
- complain.

In a report, you may have to:
- describe
- summarize.

In a proposal, you may have to:
- describe
- recommend
- summarize
- persuade.

A DETAILED STUDY

Here is a procedure for dealing with a complaint:
1 give an apology for what should (or should not) have been done
2 give an explanation or excuse for what went wrong
3 find a way of responding when you have no explanation or excuse.

1   Imagine you are the manager of Fairchild's Hotel. Use the words in brackets to provide explanations or excuses in answer to the following complaints.

    1   'Your technician seemed to have no experience of Powerpoint presentations.' (*apologize/regular technician ill*)

    2   'It was difficult to hear people using the stage microphone.' (*agree/needs replacing*)

    3   'The cashier in reception did not know which rates we had been charged.' (*speak/person concerned/misunderstanding/resolve*)

    4   'Your website took ages to load, and then crashed on us after two minutes.' (*checked/host server/assured/isolated incident*)

    5   'The vegetables at dinner were frozen, not fresh.' (*try/provide fresh vegetables in season/otherwise/good quality frozen produce*)

    6   'We were served by a foreign waiter whose English was terrible.' (*apologize/person no longer works here*)

2   Paragraphing and punctuation are important if you want your business correspondence to create a good impression. Add punctuation and paragraphing to the following:

thank you for your letter i am sorry that you were dissatisfied please accept the following explanations our regular technician was ill so the janitor who is not very experienced had to deal with the problem you had with the projector screen as to the food apart from tuesday when there was a brief power cut i do not know of any other problems in the kitchen with regard to your bill you are absolutely right you were invoiced at the peak rate i have arranged for a refund and can only apologize for the oversight despite your difficulty in accessing our website i am assured that there is not usually a problem although the error message you got often occurs when the Internet is busy i can assure you that our website functions perfectly well once again i apologize for our service where it was not up to your expectations

Now write your own answer to Part Two of the writing test. Remember to check for grammar and spelling mistakes.

LISTENING approx. 40 minutes

PART ONE

Questions 1–12

- *You will hear three telephone conversations or messages.*

- *Write **one or two words or a number** in the numbered spaces on the notes or forms below.*

Conversation One

(Questions 1–4)

- *Look at the message below.*

- *You will hear a woman calling about changing an arrangement.*

Message

To: Henry Lee

From: Maria (1) .... (Architect)

Message: Can't make Thursday's meeting about the new (2) .... It's been

rearranged for the following (3) .... at eleven. Can you make

sure you take the (4) .... document with you?

Conversation Two

(Questions 5–8)

- *Look at the note below.*

- *You will hear two people discussing a complaint.*

Message from: Freeman's about IT delivery

Following items did not arrive:

- **(5)** ....
- two printers

Delivery arrived yesterday instead of **(6)** ....

Want to know if we are willing to **(7)** .... because they had to bring in **(8)** .... from another department.

Conversation Three

(Questions 9–12)

- *Look at the message below.*

- *You will hear a woman calling about a job.*

ASTRA RECORDING COMPANY
Telephone message

While You Were Out

Caller: Sophie Clarkson

Message: Wants to know about the data input job in the **(9)**

....

Can she work **(10)** .... ? (e.g. 8 a.m.–2 p.m.)

Has some experience so needs to know if she'll get the higher

(11) .... (£9.40).

Can you get back to her on 0208 34588 before six otherwise she'll

call again **(12)** ....

PART TWO

Questions 13–22

Before you answer questions 13–22, go to pages 53–54.

Section One

(Questions 13–17)

- *You will hear five short recordings. Five people are giving advice.*

- *For each recording, decide what each speaker is giving advice about.*

- *Write one letter (**A–H**) next to the number of the recording.*

- *Do not use any letter more than once.*

13	....	**A**	writing letters
		B	making telephone calls
14	....	**C**	writing a report
15	....	**D**	making notes
		E	giving a presentation
16	....	**F**	entertaining visitors
		G	arranging a conference
17	....	**H**	going for an interview

Section Two

(Questions 18–22)

- *You will hear another five recordings. Five people are talking about a problem in a company.*

- *For each recording, decide what each speaker is talking about.*

- *Write one letter (**A–H**) next to the number of the recording.*

- *Do not use any letter more than once.*

18	....	**A**	poor sales figures
		B	inexperienced staff
19	....	**C**	poor management
20	....	**D**	staff time-keeping
		E	falling share prices
21	....	**F**	retirement of Chief Executive
		G	unsatisfactory suppliers
22	....	**H**	salary increases

EXAM INFORMATION

This part of the listening test is divided into two sections. In each section you will hear five short monologues which you have to match to a set of eight items (A–H). The set of items is linked by an overall topic or theme. The two sections each focus on different areas within a particular test. For example, one may focus on topics, the other on functions.

The topic or function will not be stated directly so you are being tested on your global listening skills and your ability to make an inference from the recording.

A DETAILED STUDY

1   Read the instructions for Section One (Questions 13–17) on page 52 and answer these questions.

    1   How many recordings will you hear?

    2   What are you specifically asked to listen out for in each recording?

    3   How many options are there?

    4   Can you select an option more than once?

2   Read through the options A–H on page 52. Which of these options probably involve:

    1   taking people out for a meal?

    2   writing a review of something?

    3   talking about your experience and qualifications?

    4   talking to someone you can't see?

Now you are ready to listen to Part Two of the listening test and answer questions 13–22.

The following exercises are best attempted when you have completed the test and checked your answers.

3   Listen to the recording for Question 13 as often as necessary to complete the gaps.

It's a good idea if you can find out in advance what their **(1)** .... are. You might think an expensive **(2)** .... out sounds **(3)** .... , but perhaps he or she may be **(4)** .... and not feel like getting dressed up and **(5)** .... somewhere posh! They might just **(6)** .... a meal in a quiet restaurant followed by an **(7)** .... night. After all they could have been **(8)** .... for hours!

4   Read through the completed text and underline the words and phrases which give you an indication that this text is option F (entertaining visitors).

5   Sometimes false clues in the text may lead you to choose the wrong option. Read the tapescript on pages 144–145 for Questions 16 and 17. Why might you confuse 'writing a report' with 'making notes'?

6   Without looking at the tapescript, put the following phrases under the correct headings.

	Writing a report	Making notes
remember to use abbreviations		
check the grammar, spelling		
it's not a good idea to use complete sentences		
who is it for, why do they want it		
try reading it aloud to someone		
use lots of space		
leave the introduction until later		
remember to use the dash		
what is the primary purpose		
try putting in words like *because, therefore, but,* or *as*		

PART THREE

Questions 23–30

- *You will hear a radio interview about how a website can help promote a business.*

- *For each question **23–30**, mark one letter (**A, B** or **C**) for the correct answer.*

23   Christine thinks the main advantage of a website for her business has been

   A   building a closer relationship with her customers.

   B   marketing to new customers around the world.

   C   saving on postage and printing of brochures.

24   What does she think is important to ask yourself before you decide to have a website?

   A   Do you want to give more information about your products?

   B   Do you want to sell your products or services online?

   C   Do you want to allow your customers to be able to check on their orders?

25   Once you have decided to have a website you should

   A   devote enough time to the project.

   B   bring in an external website designer.

   C   find out how to add new information to it.

26   What's the best way to ensure that people visit your site?

   A   Get advice from a specialist.

   B   Publish your website address on letterheads.

   C   Link your website to other websites.

27   How has the website changed Christine's approach to business?

   A   She feels comfortable with using new technology.

   B   She is able to add new products more rapidly.

   C   She runs her business entirely from her home.

28   What is her advice on managing a website?

   A   Don't do it unless you have good IT skills.

   B   Consider paying someone to update the pages.

   C   Make sure you respond to emails promptly.

29   How much has her business increased since the website went live?

   A   10 %

   B   13 %

   C   30 %

30   What does she plan to do next?

   A   Start up a new business as soon as possible.

   B   Investigate the possibility of installing broadband.

   C   Take some time to think about the future.

SPEAKING 14 minutes

PART ONE

The interview – about 3 minutes

In Part One of the speaking test, the interlocutor asks questions to each of the candidates in turn. You have to give information about yourself and express personal opinions.

Here are some questions you may be asked:

What are you studying at the moment?

What made you decide to study *(name of subject)*?

Can you tell us something about your studies?

What do you find interesting about *(name of subject)*?

Are there some aspects of the subject that you find difficult?

What do you hope to do next?

Would you like to run your own business in the future?

How helpful will your studies be to your career?

What do you like about being a student?

Are there any disadvantages about being a student?

PART TWO

Mini-presentation – about 6 minutes

In this part of the test, you are asked to give a short talk on a business topic. You have to choose one of the topics from the three below and then talk for about one minute. You have one minute to prepare your ideas.

A: WHAT IS IMPORTANT WHEN ...?

Setting up a website for your company

- Getting expert help
- Deciding who will manage the site

B: WHAT IS IMPORTANT WHEN ...?

Running your own business from home

- Keeping domestic life and work separate
- Keeping your accounts up-to-date

C: WHAT IS IMPORTANT WHEN ...?

Deciding where to relocate your company

- Checking access to transport systems
- Finding potential employees

When you have given your presentation, your partner will ask you a question about what you have said. Here are some questions they may ask you:

What did you mean when you said ...?

Can you say a bit more about what you said about ...?

A   What sort of information is useful to put on a website?

How will you let people know you have a website?

Do you think having a website is important in business?

B   Would you consider running your business from home?

What do you think is the biggest advantage/disadvantage of working from home?

What is the first thing you would do if you decided to set up a business in your own home?

C   What is good about the location of your company (or one that you know of)?

Would you mind moving to another country to work for your company?

Would you mind having a long journey to work?

Now go to pages 59–60.

EXAM INFORMATION

Part Two: The mini-presentation

In the second part of the speaking test, you have to give a mini-presentation on a business topic. You have a choice of three topics with two suggestions for each to include in your presentation. You have one minute to prepare your presentation and the presentation itself should last for about one minute. When you have finished, the other candidate asks you a question about what you have said.

This part of the test is designed to see how well you organize more extended speech. You are expected not only to give information about the topic, but to express your opinion and justify taking a particular point of view.

A DETAILED STUDY

1   Read topics A–C on page 58. Remember to:

- make good use of your preparation time to decide what you are going to say

- make a list (in your head or on paper) of the main points you want to cover

- make a note of any additional points you want to make

- speak as clearly and as naturally as possible.

2   There are lots of ways to express your opinion. For topic A, match the phrases in list 1 with those in list 2 to form complete sentences.

A   List 1

1   In my opinion it's very important to find

2   These people will know how to use

3   It could save you

4   I think you have to decide

5   If you don't do this, then you may find

6   You may find you are

List 2

a)   nobody thinks it's their responsibility.

b)   an expert to help you.

c)   who is going to manage the site at an early stage.

d)   too busy to update the site regularly.

e)   a lot of time in the long run.

f)   the technology to get the best result.

3   There are lots of ways you can add your own information. For topics B and C, match the phrases in list 1 with those in list 2 to form complete sentences.

B   List 1

1   Another important thing to do is to take

2   As well as this I would say it's important to keep

3   I also think

List 2

a)   you should pay yourself a salary.

b)   enough time off.

c)   up-to-date with the market.

C   List 1

1   It's also a good idea to make sure you can

2   And you must check that you have permission

3   In addition I would always find out

List 2

a)   to open a business there.

b)   afford the site rent.

c)   about other local businesses.

4 When your partner has finished their presentation, you have to ask them a question about what they have said. Here are some questions you could ask. Which topic (A, B or C) do you think they refer to?

A Setting up a website

B Running your own business

C Relocating a company

1 What do you think is more important, getting advice from someone who knows about this sort of thing or finding someone to look after it for you?

2 Would you like to run your own business? Why?

3 Do you think you need to understand technology to do that?

4 Are you good at figures?

5 How would you find out if there were people looking for jobs in that area?

6 How would you avoid working too hard?

7 Do you think it's essential to be near an airport?

8 What sort of information would you want to put on the home page?

9 Would you consider setting up in a rural area?

5 Now match these responses to the questions in exercise 4.

A I think it would help to have an overview of how the Internet works.

B I'd prefer to leave it to someone who really understands what they are doing.

C Hopeless! That's why I always get someone to check my budgets.

D Not really. I think I would find it too stressful at the moment.

E By making sure that I built some relaxing time into my schedule.

F Yes, I would. There are some major advantages to not living in a city.

G Just some general details about the company and how to access us.

H I think it would be a good idea to ask someone with local knowledge.

I Not necessarily, although there must be a good, alternative transport system.

Now look again at the topics in Part Two of the speaking test.

PART THREE

Discussion – about 5 minutes

In this part of the test, you are given a discussion topic. You have 30 seconds to look at this prompt card and then about 3 minutes to discuss the topic with your partner. After that the examiner will ask you more questions related to the topic.

*For **two** candidates*

Your company wants to sponsor a sports event to raise awareness of your products. You have been asked to put together a proposal about how they should do this.

Discuss the situation together, and decide:

- what type of sports event would be most suitable
- how you will promote public awareness of your products, for example, contributing to prize money, putting your brand name on sports equipment, etc.

*For **three** candidates*

Your company wants to sponsor a sports event to raise awareness of your products. You have been asked to put together a proposal about how they should do this.

Discuss the situation together, and decide:

- what type of sports event would be most suitable
- how you will promote public awareness of your products, for example, contributing to prize money, putting your brand name on sports equipment, etc.
- how you will monitor and evaluate the success of the project.

The interlocutor will then ask you some follow-up questions. Here are some questions you may be asked:

What do you think about companies sponsoring sports events?

Are there some companies who should not be involved in this sort of activity, for example, tobacco companies?

What sort of sponsoring activities do you think are most successful?

Can you give an example of commercial sponsorship and say why you think it was successful or not?

TEST THREE

READING 1 hour

PART ONE

Questions 1–7

- *Look at the statements below and the extracts from advertisements on the opposite page.*

- *Which advertisement (A, B, C or D) does each statement 1–7 refer to?*

- *For each statement 1–7, mark one letter (A, B, C or D).*

- *You will need to use some of these letters more than once.*

Example:

    0   This provider can tell you what skills you have in your company.

---

1   Training can be on your own premises or at the provider's training facility.

2   You will learn just enough of a foreign language for basic survival.

3   This provider will help you to set your own training priorities.

4   This service would be useful for people who have to represent their company at fairs and exhibitions.

5   This provider will help you get the best out of your staff.

6   This service would be useful for people who have to read technical literature written in other languages.

7   This provider can produce your promotional literature in other languages.

A

Why learn foreign languages?

Re-think your company policy on foreign language training! We offer in-house courses to meet all your needs. At Level 1, learn how to talk about yourself, your company and your work, and how to make simple business deals. At Level 2, learn to cope in meetings without interpreters. Specialist courses also available for reading technical documents, and for writing correspondence and reports.

B

Your janitor is a nuclear physicist

Well, maybe not, but you can bet there's a lot of unused talent in your company. We specialise in finding out what people can do, and what they *could* do. Our visit to you has a twofold purpose. First, we carry out an audit to determine what skills already exist in the company, together with aptitude tests to measure individual potential. Then, we carry out a company-wide audit to identify what skills the company needs. The outcome is a clear picture of training needs that allows you to invest in key training areas, e.g. an immediate improvement in sales techniques, or a longer-term investment in, say, developing language competence.

C

Do people *really* know who you are and what you do?

Let us help you update your promotional literature. Our team of specialists will help you identify your company's unique characteristics, and design your brochures accordingly, with translated versions if you need them. We are also leaders in effective website design, and will happily provide on-site training so that you can maintain your website yourselves. And if speaking in front of a large audience is a nightmare for you, we can provide top-class training in making both live and written presentations.

D

Improve your interpersonal skills!

Human Resource Development is our business. We provide flexible courses for individuals or companies at our Tutorial Centre, or, for your convenience, at your own premises at times to suit you. We cover a wide range of topics, including: getting by in a foreign language; dealing with difficult customers; making meetings more effective; holding customer loyalty and winning new customers.

PART TWO

Questions 8–12

- *Read the article below about the South African economy.*

- *Choose the best sentence from the opposite page to fill each of the gaps.*

- *For each gap 8–12, mark one letter (A–G).*

- *Do not use any letter more than once.*

- *There is an example at the beginning, (0).*

SOUTH AFRICA TODAY

South Africa is a promising business prospect. It has many resources that are just waiting to be exploited by enterprising foreign investors. The country's mineral wealth is still critical to the economy, accounting for 30 per cent of foreign exchange earnings. **(0)** ....*G*..... . It remains the country's third largest export. Platinum is the largest export commodity, followed by gold and coal, although gold's importance to the economy is lessening now that its price per ounce has dropped well below USD300.

But the South African market today is dominated by the financial services and manufacturing sectors, each contributing more than twice as much to GDP as mining. **(8)** .... The full range of services, from commercial, merchant and retail banking to mortgage lending and insurance, is provided by both local and foreign institutions. The manufacturing sector is South Africa's largest employer and represents 19 per cent of GDP. **(9)** .... Historically, manufacturing has suffered from structural weakness dating back to the protectionism of the apartheid years, which reduced its competitiveness. **(10)** .... This trend is likely to continue with the weakening of the rand.

The income from overseas visitors coming to South Africa on holiday continues to grow in importance, amounting to 10 per cent of GDP. With so many countries now affected by terrorist threats and other kinds of unrest, South Africa is regarded as a 'safe' destination. In particular, Cape Town is proving its popularity as an all-year round holiday resort. **(11)** .... In fact, the number of cruise liners which dock at Cape Town is expected to go up from the usual 10 to nearly 40 this year.

The government is also looking to eco-tourism as a major source of job creation. It is, for example, recruiting unemployed people to uproot alien vegetation (i.e. vegetation which is not native to the region). **(12)** .... Furthermore, the government has recently entered into a formal agreement with Zimbabwe and Mozambique to join together a number of game parks, which will ultimately form a 100,000 sq km game reserve to be known as Peace Park.

Example:

A   Nevertheless, manufacturing production has soared since 2000 as a result of lower interest rates, renewed economic growth and stronger demand for exports.

B   Alien plants not only absorb three million cubic metres more water a year than normal vegetation, but they also pose a serious fire risk.

C   The world-class financial sector is supported by a sound legal framework and is highly competitive.

D   Nor has the continuing fluctuation of the US dollar against the rand helped the domestic economy.

E   Tourism has received a further boost as cruise liners have been docking at South African ports in order to avoid the Suez Canal and the Middle East trouble spots.

F   It is dominated by metal and engineering, which produces 60 per cent of Africa's steel and ranks among the world's best.

G   It provides a huge market for local suppliers as well as direct employment for more than 400,000 in nearly 700 mines.

PART THREE

Questions 13–18

- *Read the article below about bullying and the questions on the opposite page.*

- *For each question 13–18, mark one letter (A, B, C or D) for the answer you choose.*

BULLYING IN THE WORKPLACE

Do you know or work with someone who undervalues other people's efforts, ignores their viewpoint, even publicly insults his or
5 her co-workers? That person is a bully and is bad news for any company, though often the people at the top don't know, or worse, don't want to know. A bully will set impossible deadlines,
10 make fun of people and ridicule them whenever they make mistakes. The worst type will also shout and be abusive. What motivates bullies? No one is sure, but it may be that they are
15 suffering from some kind of inferiority complex.

According to a recent survey, the situation is far worse than originally thought, and has become worse in the
20 past year. It's quite likely that the increase is a direct result of the current business culture with its emphasis on competition and aggressive 'masculine' management styles, combined with the
25 stress of 'job insecurity', that is, the ever-present fear of losing one's job. The survey quotes the example involving the appointment of an ageing male manager who could not come to terms with
30 women in management positions. His relationship with the mainly female staff created massive problems throughout the whole organization. The oppressive atmosphere did nothing to promote
35 efficient working practices, with stress levels rising and confidence and spirits falling. It wasn't easy for the staff to report him and it took a while to convince those at the top, but they did
40 the wise thing and got rid of him.

Bullying must be recognized and dealt with. A fair disciplinary procedure should be in place. Once a bully has been identified, employers must ensure
45 that both sides have the opportunity to make their case and be able to appeal against any disciplinary action taken.

If you work with someone who uses inappropriate or threatening language
50 or behaves in a rude and abrupt manner, you could be dealing with a bully. Whatever you do, you must not become a victim: if you do not fight back, you are giving the bully
55 encouragement to continue. On the other hand, try not to get upset, you will feel worse and the bully will be very satisfied. So, keep cool, be patient and take action when you are sure you can
60 be effective. Talk to colleagues, see what they think. Make a note of conversations, keep memos and letters, as these will be needed as evidence to back up your case. Bullies don't always
65 realize that their behaviour is offensive, upsetting and threatening, and it may be that a few well-chosen words will defuse the situation. But if this fails, the employer will have to intervene, give
70 proper warnings and be prepared to dismiss the persistent offender.

13   According to the writer, bullies are people who

    A   use cruel teasing to make other people feel inferior.

    B   enjoy upsetting people by spreading bad news.

    C   cannot get on with people of the opposite sex.

    D   believe that they are better than everyone else.

14   According to the survey, bullying has become more common recently because

    A   age and sex differences between management and staff cause tension.

    B   people are afraid they might lose their jobs if they are not strict.

    C   people feel they must be competitive and tough in order to survive.

    D   most managers prefer to ignore bullying in the workplace.

15   In the example, what effect did the bullying manager have on the company?

    A   Staff morale was very low as a result of his behaviour.

    B   He was finally dismissed when senior management realized what was happening.

    C   People felt bad about reporting him to senior management.

    D   He got on much better with male colleagues than with female colleagues.

16   To deal with bullies, there should be a proper procedure so that

    A   people who have been bullied can appeal to senior management against dismissal.

    B   both the person accused and the people accusing can put their point of view.

    C   management can dismiss anyone suspected of bullying other employees.

    D   everyone will know that the company has a definite policy on bullying.

17   If you feel you are the victim of bullying, the writer recommends that you should

    A   repay bullies by being rude and aggressive to them in turn.

    B   collect evidence to prove that the person is guilty of bullying.

    C   persuade other members of staff to support you.

    D   report the situation immediately to your supervisor.

18   What does the writer mean by the phrase 'a few well-chosen words will defuse the situation'
    lines 67–68?

    A   It's a good idea to give the bullies a list of words that people find offensive.

    B   Employers should be told very diplomatically about the bullies' behaviour.

    C   Bullies should be told that they will be sacked if the bullying doesn't stop.

    D   Bullies might change their behaviour once it is pointed out to them.

Before you check your answers, got to pages 68–69.

EXAM INFORMATION

In multiple choice questions it is important to read the text and options carefully. Sometimes the text contains:

a)   information that isn't there

A word or a phrase in the text may lead you to think it is there, but it isn't.

Look at Question 13, option D on page 67. Where does it say in the text that bullies believe they are better than everyone else?

b)   misleading expressions

A word or phrase that doesn't mean what you might think it means. Look at Question 13, option B. What does the phrase *a bully ... is bad news for any company* (lines 5–6) actually mean?

c)   confusion between definitions and examples

Use the examples to produce a definition. Look at Question 13. You are asked for a definition (*bullies are people who* ...). Which words in paragraph 1 of the text give examples of a bully's behaviour? What is the bully's purpose?

A DETAILED STUDY

1   To get a general understanding of the text, answer the following questions.

1   Which phrase in paragraph 1 describes the fact that a bully doesn't allow people enough time to do a job?

2   Which expression in paragraph 2 means that people are afraid they might be fired or made redundant?

3   Which expression in the text tells us that a male manager was unable to accept women in management positions?

4   What does the word *confidence* in line 36 mean?

5   What kind of procedure is a *disciplinary procedure* (line 42)?

6   Which expression in the text means that an accused person uses arguments to defend himself/herself?

7   What kind of language is *threatening language* (line 49)?

2   Improve your vocabulary by word building. Complete the following tables. All the words are taken from the text.

	Verb	Noun	Adjective
	satisfy	satisfaction	satisfactory
1	ignore		
2	insult		
3			abusive
4		emphasis	
5		competition	
6	create		
7			oppressive

	Verb	Noun	Adjective
8		confidence	
9	recognize		
10		action	
11		encouragement	
12			chosen
13	intervene		
14	dismiss		
15			persistent

3   The text contains a number of other words and expressions which are necessary to a complete understanding of the text. Match items 1–10 in A to the definitions (A–J) in B.

A

1   keep cool (line 58)

2   be effective (line 60)

3   inferiority complex (lines 15–16)

4   oppressive atmosphere (lines 33–34)

5   aggressive style (lines 23–24)

6   stress levels (lines 35–36)

7   inappropriate language (line 49)

8   persistent offender (line 71)

9   be abusive (lines 12–13)

10   defuse the situation (line 68)

B

A   a deep-down feeling that you are not really good at or for anything

B   saying things which do not relate or are not acceptable in a particular situation

C   an environment where you feel unable to be free or be yourself

D   act in a way that enables you to get what you want

E   shout at or insult

F   a way of behaving that attacks or ignores other people's wishes or needs

G   stay calm in a difficult situation

H   remove the danger or tension that is making everyone nervous

I   the amount of unhealthy physical or emotional pressure you are under

J   a person who keeps doing something wrong even when told not to

Now check your answers to these questions and then look back at your answers to Part Three of the reading test.

PART FOUR

Questions 19–33

- *Read the article below about industry in Brazil.*

- *Choose the best word to fill each gap from **A, B, C** or **D** on the opposite page.*

- *For each question **19–33**, mark one letter (**A, B, C** or **D**).*

- *There is an example at the beginning, (**0**).*

BRAZIL: ELECTRONIC GOODS IN TROUBLE

The home appliance and electronic goods industry is in **(0)** ....A.... ; the good years are over.

The industry enjoyed sales growth of 30% annually during the country's **(19)** .... in the nineties, but sales have been **(20)** .... fast in the last two years, and warehouses are full of unsold stock. The industry's growth **(21)** .... of 10% now looks far too optimistic.

Consumers had doubled their borrowing to $24bn in the year to May 2003. They spent much of this money on appliances, often at Brazil's three big retailers, Casas Bahia, Lojas Arapua and Ponto Frio.

Now consumers fear they have **(22)** .... their spending limits and are simply not buying anything that they don't need **(23)** ....

Thus a battle for cash buyers is **(24)** .... , and only the most efficient retail operations will handle the inevitable fall in profit **(25)** .... Arapua, which has small, specialized stores, is the company most **(26)** .... to survive the downturn in business. It will also **(27)** .... from its decision to attack the less competitive markets of the north and northeast, while Casas Bahia and Ponto Frio continue to **(28)** .... themselves to the major cities.

Suppliers, meanwhile, must **(29)** .... with warehouses that are full of goods that retailers simply don't want at the moment. Major **(30)** .... like refrigerators, cookers and washing machines are in **(31)** .... , and the problem is even worse for 'brown goods' (TVs, stereos and VCRs).

Many big-name manufacturers, including Electrolux (Sweden) and Sanyo (Japan), are looking for ways to **(32)** .... their overheads, for example, by extending holidays and cutting shifts. Their strategy is to bring costs under control, price their goods competitively and in this way stimulate the market. It looks as if the strategy is **(33)** .... : prices have fallen by 12% this year and, in the case of brown goods, by 44%.

Example:

0   **A** difficulties   **B** worries   **C** troubles   **D** problems

0	A	B	C	D

19   **A** boom   **B** profit   **C** increase   **D** value

20   **A** going   **B** dying   **C** falling   **D** sinking

21   **A** guess   **B** estimate   **C** forewarning   **D** insight

22   **A** expected   **B** caught   **C** touched   **D** reached

23   **A** eagerly   **B** urgently   **C** certainly   **D** hopefully

24   **A** expanding   **B** arriving   **C** developing   **D** fighting

25   **A** amounts   **B** margins   **C** deals   **D** losses

26   **A** sure   **B** probable   **C** expected   **D** likely

27   **A** escape   **B** recover   **C** emerge   **D** benefit

28   **A** restrain   **B** restrict   **C** contain   **D** support

29   **A** correspond   **B** compare   **C** cope   **D** compete

30   **A** objects   **B** pieces   **C** substances   **D** items

31   **A** overload   **B** overflow   **C** oversupply   **D** overrun

32   **A** reduce   **B** remove   **C** adapt   **D** adjust

33   **A** happening   **B** working   **C** winning   **D** occurring

PART FIVE

Questions 34–45

- *Read the article below about Norwich airport.*

- *In most of the lines **34–45**, there is one extra word. It is either grammatically incorrect or does not fit in with the sense of the text. Some lines, however, are correct.*

- *If a line is correct, write **CORRECT**.*

- *If there is an extra word in the line, write **the extra word** in CAPITAL LETTERS.*

- *The exercise begins with two examples, (**0**) and (**00**).*

Examples

0	C	O	R	R	E	C	T

00	I	F					

RENOVATION OF NORWICH AIRPORT

0   Norwich Airport is to have a new airport lounge dedicated to the business

00   traveller as if part of a £1.7m renovation of the terminal building due to start

34   this winter. The new business lounge will on offer longer-staying travellers a

35   place to work with PCs, faxes and satellite TV. The airport says the new changes

36   to mean business users will also benefit from a quicker service with a shorter

37   transit time from car park to airport. The renovation of the terminal building will

38   be involve improved check-in facilities with an increase in the number of desks

39   from eight to twelve, which including two desks for ticket holders with carry-on

40   luggage only. A new restaurant is planned overlooking the airport, with much

41   more shops, coffee bars and an improved washroom. Baggage handling facilities

42   are also being improved. Hugh Lawson, managing director of Norwich its Airport

43   said, 'With passenger figures expected to double over by the next ten years,

44   this redevelopment is essential.' Work on the renovation is it expected

45   to be completed by May, in no time

for the summer season.

Before you check your answers, go to page 73.

EXAM INFORMATION

Part Five of the reading test consists of a text (150–200 words) of about fifteen lines. Some of the lines have an extra word which should not be there. You have to read the text carefully in order to identify the unnecessary words. These are often words such as:

- pronouns, e.g. *it, they*
- prepositions and particles, e.g. *of, at, in, off, out*
- definers, e.g. *the, a, some, any, each, every*
- adverbs, e.g. *so, too, very*
- verb forms, e.g. *will, is, got.*

A DETAILED STUDY

1   Sometimes in the exam, two expressions are mixed up: a word is added to an expression which belongs to the word before it, but not to the word after it. For example:

*It's a place where you can usually get something **up** to drink.*

Answer: *up*

get up and *get something to drink*

Find the mixed up expressions in these sentences.

1   We were nervous because of it was a new business venture.

2   I decided to go out for to get a breath of fresh air.

3   Please type this report, and to make sure it is double-spaced.

4   This office is very stuffy. Why not don't you open the windows?

5   I see that profits are as well up on the last quarter.

6   The firm was been forced to go out of business after the worst trading figures in years.

7   There will be twelve people at the meeting that including the janitor.

8   They gave me time off to go to the hospital, so for which I was very grateful.

9   The boss had his head on the desk but he looked me up when he realized I had entered his office.

10   It's been over a month since then we last saw him!

2   Read the text and say if the following statements are true or false. Underline the part of the text that confirms your response.

1   The new business lounge will cost £1.7m.

2   The new business lounge will be situated in the terminal building.

3   The business lounge is just an area for rest and relaxation.

4   There will be a new car park closer to the airport terminal.

5   Waiting time at check-in desks should be reduced.

6   There will be separate check-in desks for people with hand luggage.

7   New facilities will include a shopping area.

8   The renovation is necessary because of an expected increase in passenger numbers.

9   The work will be completed by the end of the summer.

Now check your answers to these questions and then look back at your answers to Part Five of the reading test.

WRITING 45 minutes

PART ONE

- *The company's telephone bills are too high. As Office Manager, you need to send a memo to all staff about the use of office telephones.*

- *Write a **memo** for the attention of all staff:*

  - *telling them the situation regarding the phones*

  - *suggesting how to save money when contacting overseas customers*

  - *giving an instruction about private use of phones.*

- **Write 40–50 words**.

Memo

To: All staff
From: Office Manager
Date: 12th November
Re: Use of office telephones

Before you write your memo, go to pages 75–76.

EXAM INFORMATION

When dealing with a question in Part One of the writing test, remember to read the instructions carefully. You have to cover all the points clearly in your answer. When you have finished, check your work to make sure you have not used any unnecessary words. You must try to remain within the word limit of 40–50 words.

A DETAILED STUDY

1   Match phrases (A–L) with the instructions (1–3).

Instruction 1: tell your staff the situation regarding the phones

Instruction 2: suggest how to save money when contacting overseas customers

Instruction 3: give staff instructions about private use of phones

A   use ordinary mail for non-urgent items

B   private calls only with special permission

C   phone costs have increased greatly

D   phone during off-peak periods

E   high phone costs are unacceptable

F   use fax where possible

G   expensive overseas calls are a big element in phone costs

H   the phones are for office use only

I   all other calls must be made from the payphone

J   use email where possible

K   no personal calls except for emergencies

L   phone bills are too high

2   Read the following answer a student wrote to the question in Part One. Then answer the questions below.

> Some of you, spend too long on the phone, and it's costing the company the earth, specially overseas calls. Use email instead. Use off-peak times. Whatever. And no way should you use office phones for your private stuff, well, may be if it's an emergency, but get your supervisor's OK first.

[51 words]

1   Does it cover all the points?

2   Find one spelling mistake and two mistakes with punctuation.

3   Are phrases such as *costing ... the earth*, *And no way* or *your private stuff* appropriate here?

4   Is the language personal or impersonal? Do you think this style is appropriate for an office memo?

3   Put A–G in order to reconstruct a company memo about a problem with the cost of phone calls.

The company telephone bill for the last quarter is ...

A   calls were made to Australia and other

B   be personal calls. Any member of staff found

C   numbers given in the detailed statement shows that several

D   up by 75% over the previous quarter. An analysis of the

E   making personal calls on company phones, other

F   countries with which we do not do business. Clearly, these can only

G   than emergency calls, will be asked to cover the cost of the calls.

Now write your own answer to Part One of the writing test. Remember to check for grammar and spelling mistakes.

PART TWO

- *You work for the National Small Farmers Association. You have been asked to write a short report for NSFA members on the purchase of farm machinery.*

- *Look at the data below on which you have already made some handwritten notes.*

- *Then, using **all** your handwritten notes, write a **report** for NSFA members.*

- ***Write 120–140 words.***

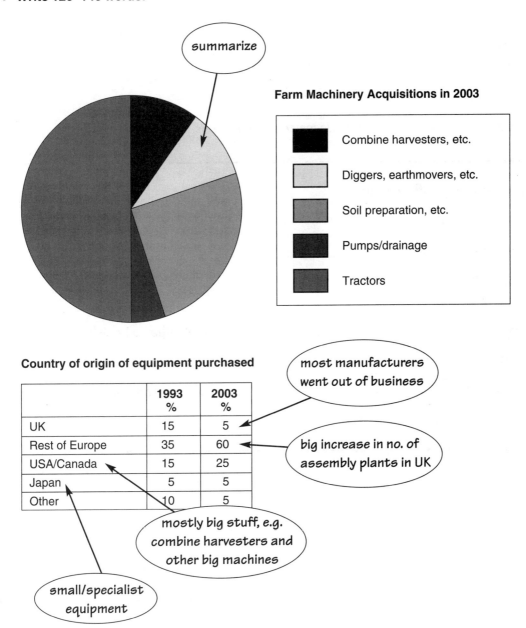

summarize

Farm Machinery Acquisitions in 2003

■	Combine harvesters, etc.
▢	Diggers, earthmovers, etc.
▨	Soil preparation, etc.
▦	Pumps/drainage
▨	Tractors

Country of origin of equipment purchased

most manufacturers went out of business

	1993 %	2003 %
UK	15	5
Rest of Europe	35	60
USA/Canada	15	25
Japan	5	5
Other	10	5

big increase in no. of assembly plants in UK

mostly big stuff, e.g. combine harvesters and other big machines

small/specialist equipment

LISTENING approx. 40 minutes

PART ONE
Questions 1–12

- *You will hear three telephone conversations or messages.*

- *Write **one or two words or a number** in the numbered spaces on the notes or forms below.*

Conversation One
(Questions 1–4)

- *Look at the note below.*

- *You will hear a woman telephoning about the despatch of some goods.*

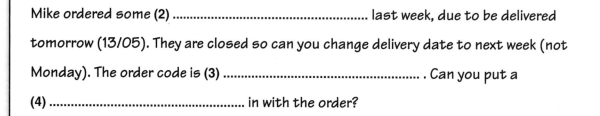

Answerphone Message

To: Katy Russell

From: Mike Ponti from (1) ....

Date: 12/05/04

Mike ordered some (2) .... last week, due to be delivered

tomorrow (13/05). They are closed so can you change delivery date to next week (not

Monday). The order code is (3) .... Can you put a

(4) .... in with the order?

Conversation Two

(Questions 5–8)

- *Look at the note below.*

- *You will hear a woman telephoning the training department of her organization.*

Message

Date:	2nd August
Time:	9.30 a.m.
From:	Louise Geller, (5) ....
Message:	She has received some information about a (6) ....
	and wants to know how much is in the (7) ....
	She thinks she needs to go on it as she's going to be the new manager at our
	West London (8) .... Can you get back to her?

Conversation Three

(Questions 9–12)

- *Look at the note below.*

- *You will hear a man calling about hiring cars.*

TELEPHONE MESSAGE

Time:	14.30
Caller:	Gerben Stoller from (9) .... Ltd.
	He is interested in our (10) .... scheme.
	Wants to know what sort of (11) .... we can offer.
	Coming into the office (12) ....

PART TWO
Questions 13–22

Section One
(Questions 13–17)

- *You will hear five short recordings. Each speaker is leaving a message for someone.*

- *For each recording, decide what the main reason for the message is.*

- *Write one letter (**A–H**) next to the number of the recording.*

- *Do not use any letter more than once.*

13	....	**A**	making an apology
		B	offering to help
14	....	**C**	asking for some information
		D	amending an order
15	....	**E**	giving instructions
16	....	**F**	cancelling an appointment
		G	making a complaint
17	....	**H**	explaining a procedure

Section Two
(Questions 18–22)

- *You will hear another five recordings. Each speaker is talking about a visitor they are expecting.*

- *For each recording, decide what sort of visitor is expected.*

- *Write one letter (**A–H**) next to the number of the recording.*

- *Do not use any letter more than once.*

18	....	**A**	Management Consultant
		B	Company Solicitor
19	....	**C**	Security Officer
20	....	**D**	Health and Safety Officer
		E	Research Officer
21	....	**F**	Human Resources Officer
		G	Training Manager
22	....	**H**	Foreign Buyer

PART THREE

Questions 23–30

Before you answer questions 23–30, go to pages 83–84.

- *You will hear an interview with a married couple who run a business together.*

- *For each question 23–30, mark one letter (A, B or C) for the correct answer.*

23   According to the interviewer, why are family-run businesses considered to be so important to the economy?

     A   They are more successful.

     B   There are more of them.

     C   Their productivity is higher.

24   According to the interviewer, how long on average does a family-run business last?

     A   15 years

     B   22 years

     C   70 years

25   What does Jill say can put a strain on a couple's relationship?

     A   working long hours

     B   sharing the same office

     C   taking too much time off

26   Why does Jill think childcare issues are not a problem for them?

     A   They no longer have young children to care for.

     B   They understand the difficulties of balancing work and family.

     C   They have agreed to share childcare responsibilities.

27   What does Scott do to help him relax?

     A   He takes the dog for a walk.

     B   He plays golf at weekends.

     C   He listens to music.

28 The only things Scott and Jill disagree about are

   A   financial matters.

   B   artistic matters.

   C   technical matters.

29 What does Scott miss about his previous job?

   A   his male colleagues

   B   eating out at lunchtime

   C   help with correspondence

30 Over the next few years Jill wants to

   A   export to other countries.

   B   take on more permanent staff.

   C   concentrate on design work.

EXAM INFORMATION

In Part Three of the listening test, you hear a longer recording which may be a conversation, a discussion, an interview or a monologue. There are eight multiple choice questions with three options for each to choose from (A–C). The questions test your ability to interpret the main ideas or details of the recording. Sometimes questions will focus on the opinions and feelings of the speakers.

A DETAILED STUDY

1   Which of these statements (1–8) can you say are true without listening to the recording?

   1   The interviewer thinks that family-run businesses are important for the economy.

   2   A family-run business usually lasts more than fifteen years.

   3   Jill thinks there are work situations which can put a strain on a couple's relationship.

   4   Jill doesn't think childcare is an issue for them.

   5   Scott listens to music to help him relax.

   6   Jill and Scott agree about most things.

   7   Scott misses the support he got in his previous job.

   8   Jill still has thoughts about what she wants to do with the business in the future.

2   Listen once and answer the following questions.

   1   How many speakers are there?

   2   Who are they?

   3   What are you listening to:

   A   a presentation?

   B   a meeting?

   C   a discussion?

3   What are the main ideas in this text? Tick any of the statements below.

   1   The contribution family-run businesses make to the country.

   2   The manufacture of high quality products.

   3   Dealing with the pressure of working long hours.

   4   Finding people to take care of the children.

   5   Ensuring that there is sufficient time to relax.

   6   Managing the finances efficiently.

   7   Avoiding potential areas of conflict.

   8   Dealing with staff problems.

   9   The disadvantages of running your own business.

   10   Plans for the future.

Now you are ready to listen to Part Three of the listening test and answer questions 23–30.

FURTHER STUDY

In order to help you listen more effectively and deal with multiple choice questions, do this exercise. You will need to look carefully at the tapescript for this part of the test on pages 148–149.

4   For each of the multiple choice questions, underline the parts of the tapescript that give you the correct answer. For Question 23, you need to understand that if something is described as *the backbone* it means it plays a central, supporting role to everything else – like the backbone in your body!

23   According to the interviewer, why are family-run businesses considered to be so important to the economy?

A   They are more successful.

B   There are more of them.

C   Their productivity is higher.

'Actually, around 70% of businesses in this country are run by families which makes them, statistically speaking, the backbone of the economy.'

SPEAKING 14 minutes

PART ONE

The interview – about 3 minutes

In Part One of the speaking test, the interlocutor asks questions to each of the candidates in turn. You have to give information about yourself and express personal opinions.

Here are some questions you may be asked:

Can you say something about where you work or study?

What do you like about the company you work for?

What disadvantages are there about your current work situation?

How do you get promotion in your business?

What aspects of studying do you find interesting?

Do you have any plans for the future?

What opportunities have you considered to increase your skills or qualifications?

How important is your job to you?

PART TWO

Mini-presentation – about 6 minutes

In this part of the test, you are asked to give a short talk on a business topic. You have to choose one of the topics from the three below and then talk for about one minute. You have one minute to prepare your ideas.

A: WHAT IS IMPORTANT WHEN ...?

Carrying out a staff review

- Strengths and weaknesses
- Training needs

B: WHAT IS IMPORTANT WHEN ...?

Promoting a new product

- Potential customers
- Unique features

C: WHAT IS IMPORTANT WHEN ...?

Choosing a suitable venue for a meeting

- Convenience
- Size of room

When you have given your presentation, your partner will ask you a question about what you have said. Here are some questions they may ask you:

What did you mean when you said ...?

Can you say a bit more about what you said about ...?

A   Do you think staff reviews are useful?

Have you ever had one and what did you think of it?

What could you learn from a staff review?

B   Do you think advertising works?

Why do you think it's important to know a lot about the product you are selling?

What aspects of product advertising do you like or dislike?

C   What would you do if the room is unsuitable?

Do you think it's important to ask people where they would like to have a meeting?

What can go wrong when you are making these sorts of arrangements?

PART THREE

Discussion – about 5 minutes

In this part of the test, you are given a discussion topic. You have 30 seconds to look at this prompt card and then about 3 minutes to discuss the topic with your partner. After that the examiner will ask you more questions related to the topic.

*For **two** candidates*

Your company has decided to produce an in-house newsletter for staff.

You have been asked to co-ordinate the project.

Discuss the situation, and decide:
- what kind of articles and information should be included
- who should be asked to contribute to the newsletter on a regular or occasional basis.

*For **three** candidates*

Your company has decided to produce an in-house newsletter for staff.

You have been asked to co-ordinate the project.

Discuss the situation, and decide:
- what kind of articles and information should be included
- who should be asked to contribute to the newsletter on a regular or occasional basis
- how often the newsletter should be produced and what it should look like.

The interlocutor will then ask you some follow-up questions. Here are some questions you may be asked:

Do you think in-house newsletters are useful? Why?

Who do you think should control the content of a newsletter?

What risks might there be in allowing staff to write letters to be published in a newsletter?

What sort of newsletter would you like to read or contribute to?

Now go to pages 88–89.

EXAM INFORMATION

Part Three: The discussion

The third part of the speaking test is a discussion between you and the other candidate(s) that lasts about three minutes. The interlocutor will sometimes continue the discussion with additional questions for a further two minutes. This part of the test is designed to check your ability to express and justify your opinion about a business-related topic. You should also be able to speculate, compare, and agree or disagree about the issues you or the other candidate(s) present.

A DETAILED STUDY

1   Read the topic below. Remember to:

- take turns to speak with your partner
- exchange ideas and suggestions with your partner
- give reasons to support your point of view
- evaluate and select ideas.

Your company has decided to produce an in-house newsletter for staff.

You have been asked to co-ordinate the project.

Discuss the situation, and decide:
- what kind of articles and information should be included
- who should be asked to contribute to the newsletter on a regular or occasional basis
- how often the newsletter should be produced and what it should look like.

---

2   Practise responding to what your partner says about the topic. Match an appropriate response (A–H) to the statements 1–8.

1   I think that we should include articles from each division.

2   I'd like to see people making suggestions about how to improve the company.

3   It would be good to advertise company training events.

4   Do you think people would like information about new members of staff?

5   I think we should get the Chief Executive to write something for the first edition.

6   We should definitely get Research and Development to let us know what they are doing.

7   I think we should have a letter page every week.

8   What about some sort of competition?

A   But they tell us about those already on the staff noticeboard.

B   Good idea. But she might not think it's important enough.

C   I agree. Ideally something from them every couple of months or so.

D   Yes, I do. People are always interested in where people have worked before.

E   Yes. It would be good to get some regular correspondence going between people.

F   I agree, but you can't force people to contribute.

G   Nice one. We'd have to get approval from management and a budget if we offer prizes.

H   It would be interesting but perhaps a bit politically sensitive?

3   Look at the comments 1–10 below and decide if they are:

    a   making a suggestion

    b   justifying an opinion

    c   evaluating an idea

    d   expressing agreement

    e   expressing disagreement.

    1   I accept what you're saying.

    2   I think there's something in what you say.

    3   What about including an editorial?

    4   That's not how I see it.

    5   I think it's going to be cheaper that way.

    6   Let's have a closer look at your suggestion.

    7   Absolutely!

    8   Why don't we make a proposal?

    9   I don't believe that.

    10   It's the only way we can get them to agree with us.

4   Complete this dialogue using an appropriate comment from 1–10 in exercise 3.

Man: I think we should aim to get the newsletter out at least every month.

Woman: **(1)** .... But it's going to be a lot of work.

Man: What do you mean?

Woman: Trying to get people to submit articles regularly.

Man: **(2)** .... Anyway, we don't have to depend on people writing articles all the time. We can have letter pages and competitions and so on.

Woman: Well, **(3)** .... so I think we need to discuss it with management first.

Man: Right then. **(4)** ....?

Now look again at the prompt cards in Part Three of the speaking test.

TEST FOUR

READING 1 hour

PART ONE

Questions 1–7

- *Look at the statements below and the office notices on the opposite page.*

- *Which office notice (**A, B, C** or **D**) does each statement **1–7** refer to?*

- *For each statement **1–7**, mark one letter (**A, B, C** or **D**).*

- *You will need to use some of these letters more than once.*

Example:

    0   Keep a record of what you use.

---

1   You are allowed only one hour for this.

2   Tell the appropriate person if something goes wrong.

3   Tell the person in charge if anyone is not at work on that day.

4   Tell your boss before you go to this place.

5   These are the periods when you must be at your place of work.

6   This is something you must do before you leave your work station.

7   This is not for your own private use.

A

Flexible working hours

Employees may start work at any time between 07.00 and 09.30, and finish not earlier than 16.30 and not later than 18.00. The lunch break must be taken between 12.00 and 14.00. Thus, 'block times' (i.e. when all employees are in) are 09.30–12.00 and 14.00–16.30. Three breaks are permitted during the working day: sixty minutes for lunch and two other ten minute breaks, the timing of which must be agreed with your immediate superior.

B

Fire Drill

There will be a fire drill at 10.30 on the second Tuesday of every month.

When you hear the fire alarm, immediately stop what you are doing. Close any open windows and close the door behind you, then walk, don't run, to the assembly point outside the building (see map).

Report to the Fire Drill Officer and inform him/her if any of your colleagues are absent.

Do not re-enter the building until you are told to do so.

C

Use of Sick Room

The Sick Room is only to be used in genuine cases of illness or injury.

If you are ill or have an accident, inform your immediate superior before going to the Sick Room.

Do not try to use the Sick Room equipment yourself: that is the Nurse's responsibility.

Normally, a visit to the Sick Room should not last more than thirty minutes.

In serious cases, employees will be sent or taken to hospital.

D

Rules for use of photocopier

Please enter in the log the following information every time you use the photocopier: time and date, name, department, number of passes and sheets of paper used.

Use of the machine for copying personal documents is strictly forbidden.

In the event of a breakdown, switch off the machine and inform the Office Manager immediately.

Make sure that the paper tray is loaded before and after you use the machine.

PART TWO

Questions 8–12

- *Read the article below about Speech Recognition (SR), i.e. computer programs that can recognize spoken language.*

- *Choose the best sentence from the opposite page to fill each of the gaps.*

- *For each gap **8–12**, mark one letter (**A–G**).*

- *Do not use any letter more than once.*

- *There is an example at the beginning, (**0**).*

SPEECH RECOGNITION

Speech recognition (SR) is the method by which you can talk to a computer to bring words up on the screen. It may have been an American invention, but several European software companies have developed some wonderful SR software. The idea is not new – but it did take the business world a long time to catch up with it. **(0)** ....*G*..... .

The new products are so amazing that four years ago, IBM's speech recognition program was at the top of the software-sales charts for several weeks, even beating the most popular computer games of the time.

Recognizing words and turning them into text may seem magic in itself, but it is even cleverer than that. If you pay close attention, you will notice that the system waits a fraction of a second before the words come up. **(8)** .... In other words, whatever you say, the system checks the two words before it and the two words after it.

(9) .... For example, in English, if you dictate *right away*, it will look at the context of the other words to work out if you mean *write away* or *right away*. This means you should be able to say, 'Please write to Mr Wright right away.' and the screen will show it correctly.

At first, users had to sit in front of their desktop computer to use their SR program. **(10)** .... One company, Grundig, is now marketing a handheld portable dictation machine which will connect with a PC and send a spoken report directly into Dragon's Naturally Speaking SR program. These modern systems not only translate your speech into screen text, but they do so remarkably quickly. **(11)** .... An experiment using a television newsreader achieved a speed of 120 words per minute. The program Voice Express claims a speed of 140 words per minute is possible.

(12) .... Virtually every instruction you click on in a Microsoft drop-down menu can be spoken: say, 'New item' and a new file opens. It is even possible, though a bit more complicated, to set up an address book on your computer: you just say a person's name and their address comes up automatically! It will soon be possible to say, 'Email to Smith', and the computer will automatically open the email software and type in Smith's email address. In fact, one company has already applied SR techniques to the telephone: you speak someone's name into the phone and it calls their number!

Example:

```
0 | A  B  C  D  E  F  G
```

A   This is to see if it makes statistical sense, that is, to assess which combination of the words is most probable and how likely it is that they would appear in this context.

B   And because women generally speak more clearly than men, speeds for women are even faster.

C   There is a very good reason for that moment of hesitation: the system knows how words go together!

D   They can even cope with English spoken by Parisians, Italians or south Londoners, who all talk very fast.

E   What is even more exciting is that modern systems can now take spoken words as commands to the computer.

F   Now, all the major producers have brought in ways of allowing business users to dictate to their laptop and send their words back to the office.

G   Dragon Systems invented it as far back as 1984, and although a one-person system cost £32,000 eight years ago, there are now excellent SR software packages available for as little as £30.

Before you check your answers, go to pages 94–95.

A DETAILED STUDY

1   Answer the following questions to help you with the general meaning of the text.

    1   Where was speech recognition (SR) first invented?

    2   Why does the writer say that the new SR software products are *amazing*? (paragraph 2)

    3   Why does the system wait *a fraction of a second* before writing your spoken words?

    4   How does a handheld portable dictation machine transmit its material?

    5   How do SR programs handle commands?

    6   How does an address book on your computer work with an SR program?

2   Now look at items A–G and answer the questions. This exercise helps you to relate the items to their proper place in the text. (Remember, one item does not belong in the text.)

    A   *This* is to see if it makes statistical sense ...
         What does the word *This* refer back to?

    B   *And* because women ...
         What does the word *And* refer back to?

    C   There is a very good reason for *that* moment of hesitation ...
         Which moment?

    D   *They* can *even* cope with ...
         Who are *They*? What does the word *even* refer back to?

    E   What is even *more exciting* ...
         More exciting than what?

    F   *Now,* all the major producers have brought in ways ...
         The writer is contrasting the present situation with what earlier situation?

    G   Dragon Systems invented *it* ...
         Invented what?

3   Remember, ideas are always linked by a word or words which refer back (and sometimes forward) to something in the text. Complete the following sentences with an appropriate word.

    1   I hate being in debt. .... is why I always pay all my bills on time.

    2   The auditors spent four weeks checking the company's books. .... even asked to look at the boss's personal accounts.

    3   Losing our best engineer was bad enough, but it was even .... when the CEO resigned.

    4   When the company went bankrupt, the bailiffs took all the office equipment. They .... took the coffee machine!

    5   There are two reasons why the firm changed working hours, and the unions are happy to accept .... of them.

6   There are two things you must do to improve security: ...., fit better locks on all the doors and windows; ...., install CCTV.

7   .... does the program recognize standard English, but it can also cope with regional accents.

8   The company ran at a loss for the first three years, mainly .... of the interest payments on its business loan.

9   What is the difference .... a bill and an invoice?

10   The new SR program is very fast, but .... is not really suited to our business needs.

4   Put A–G in order to reconstruct an article about job-sharing.

The biggest employment advance of recent years is what so many career-minded mothers have wanted for decades: half a job. Half a real job, that is, with all the advantages, pay rises and prospects that go ...

A   accumulating a lot of money when there are things they would both much rather be doing.

B   from a childless senior computer worker who is seeking to share his job simply to improve his quality of life. The computer worker explained that he and his wife had both been working for years and felt there was not much sense in

C   with a full-time career, in return for an investment of half the hours and half the responsibility. More and more companies are beginning to realize

D   from the other half of the team on all that has happened in her absence. But, however well skills and time priorities have been matched, the success of a job-share depends to a large extent

E   that it is better to have a good employee on her own terms than not to have her at all. Jobs can be

F   on the chemistry of its sharers. If there is suspicion or jealousy instead of trust, or if their work styles vary, inconsistency may set in and efficiency will suffer. Job-sharing isn't only popular with working mothers. British Airways recently received an appeal

G   shared in many ways: alternate weeks, mornings or afternoons. But however the scheme is organized, the most important part of the job-sharer's week is the handover period, when a job-sharer gets a crucial update

Now check your answers to these questions and then look back at your answers to Part Two of the reading test.

PART THREE

Questions 13–18

- *Read the article below about leadership and the questions on the opposite page.*

- *For each question 13–18, mark one letter (A, B, C or D) for the answer you choose.*

STARTING UP A BUSINESS: SERVICE AND MANUFACTURING SECTORS COMPARED

Starting up a business is easier in the service sector than in manufacturing. A new manufacturer has to invest heavily in factory premises, machinery and staff whereas a service
5 sector start-up requires a much smaller initial investment. However, these new service sector firms often take a long time to build up a client base. They rely heavily on word of mouth to attract customers, a slow process that causes a
10 few uncomfortable months while waiting for customers to arrive. With few customers, cash flow is minimal, but the start-up bank loan still has to be serviced, and there may be promotional costs like price cuts or free
15 samples.

In contrast, new manufacturers have to find more start-up capital. They take the risk of a high initial investment only because they know there is a ready market for their product. On
20 the other hand, the service sector start-up is more speculative, based on the hope that people will want the service offered, so payback may be seriously delayed. But service sector start-ups have one big advantage over
25 manufacturing. A restaurant, for example, could be set up in a few weeks, enough time to find premises, buy equipment 'off the shelf' and recruit staff. A manufacturer, on the other hand, needs about a year to find suitable premises,
30 install machinery and make deals with suppliers of materials. This delays the time taken for cash inflows to start offsetting the start-up costs for the manufacture.

Cash flow is also influenced by the way
35 demand may vary according to the time of year. Many manufacturers face a seasonal pattern of demand for their product, but the

seasonality is more acute for many service sector firms. Manufacturers can produce stock
40 before their seasonal peak, thus allowing them to spread the pressure on the production process. But for service providers who make most of their money during one peak period, seasonality increases the level of risk. If the peak
45 season fails, e.g. ice cream sales crash because of a cold summer, the whole business could collapse before the next peak season.

Even more importantly, service providers have to respond instantly to changes in
50 customer demand. Any variation, whether caused by seasonal factors or changes in fashion, hits service providers immediately. This implies an even greater need for a market-oriented approach by service providers. There
55 is, however, a positive aspect for service firms: unlike manufacturers, they are less likely to be caught with huge stocks of unwanted products.

A firm's financial success depends on adding value to its products, that is, selling its products
60 at a price that is higher than the cost of making them. In setting a price, companies must ensure that their customers believe that the product or service is worth the price being charged. This is harder for service providers. Customers can
65 calculate more or less the cost of providing a restaurant meal or painting a room. It's much harder to judge the cost of manufacturing products like cars or refrigerators. Thus, service providers have to work much harder to add
70 value to their services while avoiding any suspicion of overcharging. The implication of this is that manufacturers are likely to find it easier to trade with higher profit margins than service sector firms.

13   Why is a service business easier to start up than a manufacturing business?

   A   It needs less capital to set up the business.

   B   It is more aware of what its customers want.

   C   It has no difficulty finding trained staff.

   D   It depends on personal recommendation.

14   New service sector businesses may face a cash flow problem because they

   A   have to reduce prices in order to attract customers.

   B   cannot always get a big enough loan from their bank.

   C   have used most of their capital to set up the business.

   D   may not have an immediate demand for their services.

15   Variation in demand is not usually a problem for manufacturers because they

   A   need less cash once the initial investment has been made.

   B   know that there is a steady market for their product.

   C   can use off-peak periods to build up stocks of their product.

   D   are able to reduce their prices to encourage sales in off-peak periods.

16   The phrase 'market-oriented approach' (lines 53–54) means that service providers must

   A   promote their business through advertising.

   B   be aware of their customers' changing needs.

   C   keep a tight control over their cash flow situation.

   D   take care to maintain a balance between costs and profits.

17   Why do manufacturers suffer when customer demand disappears?

   A   They cannot respond quickly to changes in the market.

   B   They make most of their money in peak periods like Christmas.

   C   They might have a lot of stock that they cannot sell.

   D   They have to keep to very strict budgets.

18   Manufacturers trade with higher profit margins because

   A   their initial investment is higher so they need a higher return.

   B   their customers are unaware of the costs involved in manufacturing.

   C   their costs include a much higher budget for advertising and promotion.

   D   their products are generally more expensive to make.

PART FOUR

Questions 19–33

- *Read the article below about the use of energy in commercial buildings.*

- *Choose the best word to fill each gap from **A, B, C** or **D** on the opposite page.*

- *For each question **19–33**, mark one letter (**A, B, C** or **D**).*

- *There is an example at the beginning, (**0**).*

A WASTE OF ENERGY

The amount of energy consumed – and wasted – in commercial
buildings is increasing all the time. The **(0)** ....Å..... in numbers of
items of electronic office equipment threatens to reach its
maximum in our main business centres in the next ten years.
Office staff leave equipment **(19)** .... on unnecessarily for a
number of reasons. These include fear of **(20)** .... the
machine, **(21)** .... of knowledge of the actual cost of running
the machine, and just plain laziness.

(22) .... to control the energy usage of office equipment is wasteful, and can
(23) .... to costs far higher than most managers **(24)** .... The Energy Efficiency
and **(25)** .... Authority (EECA) is introducing a two-fold programme aimed at
(26) .... the $55m which is wasted every year in the country's offices. Office
machines consume 400 GWh of energy per year, or about 1.5% of the country's
(27) .... electricity consumption.

Further, the EECA now **(28)** .... that the number of office machines will double
before the end of the decade. By this time, office machinery energy consumption is
(29) .... to be about 800 GWh per year. A recent survey of offices in the capital city's
central business **(30)** .... revealed that 40% of office equipment was left **(31)** ....
overnight and through the weekend, as well as in working hours. It also found that
about half the energy consumed during office hours is wasted, because machines
remain on when not in **(32)** .... In particular, most PCs, printers and photocopiers
are fully **(33)** .... for only about 40% of a working day.

Example:

    0   **A** growth   **B** count   **C** progress   **D** result

0	A	B	C	D
	▬	▭	▭	▭

---

19 **A** driven   **B** switched   **C** remained   **D** stayed

20 **A** hurting   **B** offending   **C** damaging   **D** spoiling

21 **A** lack   **B** need   **C** want   **D** gap

22 **A** Neglect   **B** Prevention   **C** Loss   **D** Failure

23 **A** come   **B** take   **C** keep   **D** lead

24 **A** decide   **B** realize   **C** explain   **D** produce

25 **A** Conservation   **B** Contraction   **C** Conversion   **D** Conference

26 **A** sparing   **B** controlling   **C** saving   **D** removing

27 **A** same   **B** whole   **C** total   **D** all

28 **A** estimates   **B** proposes   **C** foretells   **D** guesses

29 **A** told   **B** expected   **C** awaited   **D** argued

30 **A** environment   **B** district   **C** region   **D** section

31 **A** circulating   **B** going   **C** playing   **D** running

32 **A** place   **B** work   **C** use   **D** time

33 **A** exercised   **B** operated   **C** handled   **D** utilized

PART FIVE

Questions 34–45

- Read the article below about websites and search engines.

- In most of the lines **34–45**, there is one extra word. It is either grammatically incorrect or does not fit in with the sense of the text. Some lines, however, are correct.

- If a line is correct, write **CORRECT**.

- If there is an extra word in the line, write **the extra word** in CAPITAL LETTERS.

- The exercise begins with two examples, **(0)** and **(00)**.

Examples

0	C	O	R	R	E	C	T

00	T	H	A	T			

WEBSITES AND SEARCH ENGINES

0   You log on to the Internet because you want to find out more about, say,

00   helicopters. So that you use a search engine like Google and type in the word

34   *helicopter*. You will have 'hits' pointing you to a lots of different websites.

35   Easy. But, let us say that if your company, Poppycock plc, has a website and

36   you want to make sure that people can find you, so you are type in *poppycock*,

37   and your company isn't there. What went wrong? The whole point of having a

38   website is that search engines which should be able to find it, and potential

39   customers should be able to make up contact. But if a site is not correctly

40   designed, a search engine will either not find it or will refuse to list it. As far

41   away as new customers are concerned, it might as well not exist. Unfortunately,

42   this element of website design is not yet generally understood, at the least in the

43   UK. Imagine printing a new brochure and then by leaving copies sitting in a box

44   in an office cupboard. Many websites are just as also inaccessible. Sadly, even

45   when some website designers do not yet understand the importance of Internet

         marketing, and so fail to ensure that your website will appear.

Before you check your answers, go to page 101.

A DETAILED STUDY

Sometimes the exam tests phrases which may or may not contain the word *the*, particularly phrases with the pattern verb + noun, e.g. *take place*, and preposition + noun, e.g. *for instance*.

1   These sentences contain phrases with the pattern verb + (*the*) + noun. Underline the word *the* if it is not necessary.

    1   I'll be in the touch as soon as I have more information for you.

    2   The good weather won't last, so make the most of it!

    3   Always tell the truth – unless you have a very good memory!

    4   Never make the fun of your subordinates, especially in front of other people.

    5   Why does the boss need such a fancy car? It must have cost the earth!

    6   It's a pleasure to do the business with you.

    7   Do you remember the man who couldn't come to the terms with women bosses?

    8   I have explained to everyone why we need to move the premises, but I am not sure everyone gets the point.

    9   Don't worry about the mess. I'll take the care of it.

    10   I shall say this only once, so please pay the attention to what I am saying.

    11   If you break the rules, sooner or later you will have to pay the price.

    12   By reducing prices, you might get more business, but you also run the risk of getting into financial difficulties.

2   These sentences contain phrases with the pattern preposition + (*the*) + noun. Put in the word *the* where necessary.

    1   The firm has had a really bad year, so pay increases are out of .... question.

    2   Every day, at .... least six of our machines are out of .... order. It isn't good enough!

    3   If people want quality, they have to pay for it. The price increases we have introduced may lose a few customers at .... first, but my guess is that in .... long run we will outperform our competitors.

    4   Officially, I am supposed to say that everything is fine, but off .... record, the company is in .... serious trouble.

    5   Everyone has worked really hard, and I want to thank the sales staff in .... particular for their efforts.

    6   There have been a few problems with the start-up, but nothing out of .... ordinary.

    7   The premises burnt down so we had to start the business again from .... scratch.

    8   Because of the downturn in business, everyone will be on a three-day week until .... further notice.

    9   Our mission statement is very important: everyone should know it by .... heart.

    10   Your spelling is terrible. You even spell your own name incorrectly! Do you do it on .... purpose?

    11   Take these packages to Deptford, and call in at Head Office on .... way.

Now check your answers to these questions and then look back at your answers to Part Five of the reading test.

WRITING 45 minutes

PART ONE

- *You are a hotel manager, and a school leaver is joining your hotel to gain work experience.*

- *Write a **note** to your staff:*

  - *giving them brief details about her*

  - *suggesting which departments she should work in*

  - *asking them for help with the report you will have to write on her.*

- ***Write 40–50 words.***

From:	Hotel Manager
To:	All staff
Date:	19th September
Re:	School leaver on work experience

PART TWO

- *Your boss wants to relocate his factory to another town, and has sent you a memo telling you the information he needs.*

- *You have visited the town and have written notes on a copy of the town map.*

- *Then using **all** your handwritten notes and the boss's memo, write a **report** on your findings.*

- ***Write 120–140 words.***

MEMO

These are the main points to investigate:

- location (check out the Westside Industrial Estate)
- communications (road and rail)
- housing (cost, availability)
- any government/EU grants available.

If you can, try to find out wage costs.

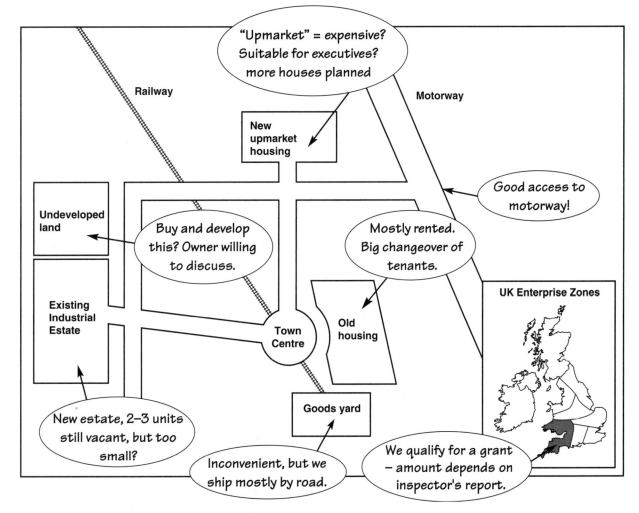

Before you write your report, go to page 104.

EXAM INFORMATION

When dealing with a question in Part Two of the writing test, make sure you read through the information carefully and understand all the details.

A DETAILED STUDY

1   Read the handwritten notes in Part Two again and answer these questions.

    1   What do the notes say about the Westside Industrial Estate?

    2   What do they say about the piece of land adjoining the Industrial Estate?

    3   How does the factory usually transport goods?

    4   What do the notes say about the housing around the town centre?

    5   What do they say about the upmarket housing?

    6   Why is the firm eligible for a grant if it moves to the town?

2   Read this sample report and comment on items 1–8. For each item, ask yourself the question, *Has the report writer given enough information?* and make changes where necessary.

---

[1] Westfield Industrial Estate has some places, [2] but maybe we would have a problem fitting into them. [3] We could use the field next to it. [4] There's a motorway and a railway. [5] There's a lot of old but good workers' housing near the centre and there are always properties to rent or buy. [6] There's also some upmarket housing. [7] The town is in an Enterprise Zone, and we might get a grant. [8] It's a good town.

Now write your own answer to Part Two of the writing test. Remember to check for grammar and spelling mistakes.

LISTENING approx. 40 minutes

PART ONE

Questions 1–12

Before you answer questions 1–12, go to page 110.

- *You will hear three telephone conversations or messages.*

- *Write **one or two words, a date or a number** in the numbered spaces on the notes or forms below.*

Conversation One

(Questions 1–4)

- *Look at the form below.*

- *You will hear a man talking to an employment agency.*

**ProPlan
Employment**

Date: 15/8/04

Time: 13.15

Caller: Piet Morganson

Company: Harris International [**(1)** .... manufacturer]

Day required: from 22nd August

Skills/Qualifications: good/expert **(2)** ....

Special requirements: must be willing to work occasional **(3)** ....

Number of staff required: (4) ....

Conversation Two

(Questions 5–8)

- *Look at the form below.*

- *You will hear a woman talking to the catering manager of her organization.*

Catering Department

Week: 10–14 June

Day required: (5) ....

Service: (6) Variety of .... and dessert.

Number of guests: 12

Location: (7) ....

Division: (8) .... Contact name: Francesca Wilks

Conversation Three

(Questions 9–12)

- *Look at the page from a diary below.*

- *You will hear two people discussing arrangements.*

Week 41	October

Monday 10

Meeting with Engel and Volker at (9) ....

Tuesday 11

Visitors arriving from (10) .... at 6 p.m.
Dinner at Gino's restaurant.

Wednesday 12

Out of office
(11) Finish ....

Thursday 13

2 p.m.: Meeting with C.E. to discuss (12) ....

Friday 14

AGM (all day)

Saturday 15

Sunday 16

PART TWO

Questions 13–22

Before you answer questions 13–22, go to page 110.

Section One
(Questions 13–17)

- *You will hear five short recordings.*

- *For each recording, decide what sort of service the company offers.*

- *Write one letter (**A–H**) next to the number of the recording.*

- *Do not use any letter more than once.*

13	....	**A**	management consultancy
		B	website design
14	....	**C**	insurance
		D	banking
15	....	**E**	catering
16	....	**F**	advertising
		G	travel
17	....	**H**	telecommunications

Section Two
(Questions 18–22)

- *You will hear another five recordings.*

- *For each recording, decide what each speaker is giving advice about.*

- *Write one letter (**A–H**) next to the number of the recording.*

- *Do not use any letter more than once.*

18	....	**A**	product design
		B	office furniture
19	....	**C**	staff development
20	....	**D**	overtime
		E	shift patterns
21	....	**F**	interviews
		G	flexitime
22	....	**H**	presentations

PART THREE

Questions 23–30

Before you answer questions 23–30, go to page 111.

- *You will hear a man talking about the best ways to get financial support for a new business.*

- *For each question 23–30, mark one letter (A, B or C) for the correct answer.*

23   How long had the man's business been running when he decided to expand?

   A   a few months

   B   two years

   C   six years

24   Why did he choose Business Angels?

   A   They have a very good reputation.

   B   They offer their experience as well as cash.

   C   They had helped him in the past.

25   How did he know where to go for funding?

   A   His bank manager told him about the scheme.

   B   He had learnt about the scheme at university.

   C   His family had previous knowledge of the scheme.

26   What did the funding selection process involve?

   A   asking relevant questions

   B   researching the competition

   C   producing a business plan

27   The result of the process was an offer of

   A   more than he had expected to receive.

   B   enough to fund an advertising campaign.

   C   not sufficient to achieve his original goals.

28 After receiving the funding, John Hamilton

    A opened new retail outlets.

    B developed his product range.

    C instigated a publicity drive.

29 In return for their funding, Business Angels expect to receive

    A shares in the company.

    B control of the business.

    C a proportion of the profits.

30 What has made private investors consider funding small businesses?

    A There is uncertainty in the financial market.

    B The rewards are likely to be high.

    C They can exert influence over the business.

A DETAILED STUDY

Part One

This exercise helps to show you what type of information you should listen for.

1   Read carefully through the forms for Conversations 1 and 2, and the diary for Conversation 3. Decide what sort of word fits each gap. Choose from the list below.

---

an activity   a day of the week   a skill   a department   a time   a number
a topic   a type of food   a product   a room   a shift   a country

---

2   Were any gaps difficult to guess? Why?

Now you are ready to listen to Part One of the listening test and answer questions 1–12.

Part Two

3   This exercise helps you to focus on the relevant details. Listen to the five recordings for Section 1. Decide if the following statements are true or false.

		True	False
Question 13			
A	This business employs mostly attractive, young people with good marketing skills.	☐	☐
B	This business advises companies on how best to use new technologies.	☐	☐
Question 14			
A	This industry is dependent on a healthy financial climate.	☐	☐
B	This industry has been affected by poor weather in Spain.	☐	☐
Question 15			
A	A lot of people resent paying for what this industry offers.	☐	☐
B	This industry is more concerned with big business than the general public.	☐	☐
Question 16			
A	This company employs six consultants.	☐	☐
B	This company offers a form of advice.	☐	☐
Question 17			
A	This company can help businesses to run more efficiently.	☐	☐
B	This company offers to reduce the risk of security leaks.	☐	☐

4   Read through the options A–H. Without listening to the recording, match the extracts (1–5) to the appropriate option (A–H).

   A   product design

   B   office furniture

   C   staff development

   D   overtime

   E   shift patterns

   F   interviews

   G   flexitime

   H   presentations

   1   I think most of the work stations in this office are really badly designed.

   2   The last thing you want a potential new employer to think is that you're unreliable.

   3   … it allows individuals to come up with a personal training programme for themselves.

   4   Now I know there are core times when everyone is supposed to be in the office.

   5   … we can avoid paying double time on a Saturday afternoon and even more for a Sunday.

Now you are ready to listen to Part Two of the listening test and answer questions 13–22.

Part Three

5   Listen to the recording for Part Three once. Can you complete the following sentences?

   1   John Hamilton is the .... of a company.

   2   When he went into business he had to depend on his .... and ....

   3   He knew there wasn't much point in asking his .... to lend him money.

   4   Business Angels are groups of .... people who can lend your business money.

   5   They do this for a .... in your company.

Now you are ready to listen to Part Three of the listening test and answer questions 23–30.

SPEAKING 14 minutes

PART ONE

The interview – about 3 minutes

In Part One of the speaking test, the interlocutor asks questions to each of the candidates in turn. You have to give information about yourself and express personal opinions.

Here are some questions you may be asked:

Do you have a job or are you studying?

Could you tell me something about the work that you do?

What sort of company would you like to work for?

Have you a preference about the sort of business you would like to be in?

How easy is it to get promotion in your company?

How long do you plan on staying in your present position?

Have you thought about what sort of career you would like?

Does working in a foreign country appeal to you?

PART TWO

Mini-presentation – about 6 minutes

In this part of the test, you are asked to give a short talk on a business topic. You have to choose one of the topics from the three below and then talk for about one minute. You have one minute to prepare your ideas.

A: WHAT IS IMPORTANT WHEN ...?

Organizing business travel

- Check dates and times carefully
- Cost-effectiveness

B: WHAT IS IMPORTANT WHEN ...?

Making changes to work shifts

- Consult staff
- Discuss effects changes may have

C: WHAT IS IMPORTANT WHEN ...?

Dealing with a complaint from a customer

- Collect information
- Interview those concerned

When you have given your presentation, your partner will ask you a question about what you have said. Here are some questions they may ask you:

What did you mean when you said ...?

Can you say a bit more about what you said about ...?

A   What do you think about business travel?

Do you think travelling on business is a waste of company money?

Would you like to travel on business? Why?

B   What are the disadvantages and advantages of working shifts?

How would you feel if your shift pattern was changed?

Do you think people should be paid more for working shifts? Why?

C   Do you think staff need training to deal with complaints?

What do you think is the best way to handle a complaint?

Is the customer always right?

PART THREE

Discussion – about 5 minutes

In this part of the test, you are given a discussion topic. You have 30 seconds to look at this prompt card and then about 3 minutes to discuss the topic with your partner. After that the examiner will ask you more questions related to the topic.

*For **two** candidates*

You would like to go on a presentation course which means you have to take a week off work. You need to convince your line manager that the course will benefit the company as well as yourselves.

Discuss the situation together, and decide:

- in what way the course will benefit the company
- why you feel that the course is particularly suited to your needs at the present time.

---

*For **three** candidates*

You would like to go on a presentation course which means you have to take a week off work. You need to convince your line manager that the course will benefit the company as well as yourselves.

Discuss the situation together, and decide:

- in what way the course will benefit the company
- why you feel that the course is particularly suited to your needs at the present time
- how your work can be covered while you are away.

The interlocutor will then ask you some follow-up questions. Here are some questions you may be asked:

Do you think staff development is important? Why?

Do you think employees should only go on courses which can also benefit the company?

What preparations would you make before you went on a course?

What sort of courses do you think staff can benefit from?

Now go to pages 115–116.

EXAM INFORMATION

Further practice for Part Three

In Part Three of the speaking test, you have to show that you can express opinions, compare and contrast ideas, concede points and, when appropriate, reach a conclusion about the topic of conversation. The interlocutor will sometimes join in and extend the discussion with questions of their own.

Be prepared to:

- agree or disagree with your partner or the interlocutor
- compare or contrast the ideas being expressed
- respond appropriately to your partner's input
- respond appropriately to the interlocutor's questions.

A DETAILED STUDY

1   Read the topic. Then match the questions in list A below with the responses in list B.

> You would like to go on a presentation course which means you have to take a week off work. You need to convince your line manager that the course will benefit the company as well as yourselves.
>
> Discuss the situation together, and decide:
>
> - in what way the course will benefit the company
> - why you feel that the course is particularly suited to your needs at the present time.

List A

1   What is the company going to gain from this course?

2   What do you need to know about giving presentations?

3   Why do you think you need to go on this course at the moment?

4   What are you going to do about your work while you're away?

5   Won't you get very behind with your work?

6   Do you think staff development is important?

7   Do you think staff should only go on courses which benefit the company?

8   What preparations would you make before you went on a course?

9   What sort of courses do you think staff can benefit from?

List B

A   Any sort really, provided they are relevant to them.

B   Because I have been asked to talk about our new product range at a sales conference in the spring.

C   I'm going to see if I can get someone to cover for me.

D   Not if I plan things carefully.

E   Not necessarily. They can improve staff morale.

F   First of all I'd make sure that people knew when I was away and for how long.

G   I think I'll be able to increase sales significantly.

H   Yes, I do. It stimulates people and you get higher productivity from them.

I   Lots. I want to be able to communicate better.

2   It is a good idea to show the interlocutor you have reached the end of your discussion. Complete sentences 1–5 below with an appropriate phrase (a–e).

   a   So, shall we agree to

   b   Right, so you think

   c   So, if we can just summarize

   d   So if I've understood correctly, we've decided you

   e   Can we agree that

1   .... that the company would be losing out if you didn't go on this course.

2   .... would go on this course if there was someone to cover for you?

3   .... staff development is not going to make much difference to our productivity?

4   .... disagree on that particular issue?

5   .... – there's not going to be a problem as long as we make reasonable preparations for your absence.

Now look again at the prompt cards in Part Three of the speaking test.

KEY AND EXPLANATION

TEST ONE

pp.6–7   READING Part 1

0   **D**   Refers to the words *applicant will be bilingual.*

1   **A**   Refers to the words *Send CV with covering handwritten letter.*

2   **C**   Refers to the words *a degree in … biology or chemistry.*

3   **D**   Refers to the words *For further details and an application form, phone or write to …*

4   **A**   Refers to the words *details of current salary.*

5   **B**   Refers to the words *to take charge of* and *working as part of the management team.*

6   **A**   Refers to the words *a one-year contract renewable.*

7   **D**   The ad only mentions being bilingual and at least three years' relevant experience.

FURTHER PRACTICE AND GUIDANCE (pp.8–9)

1   **1**   Shop D: Both A and D sell fresh vegetables, but only D accepts credit cards.
   2   Shops A, B or D: They are all open Wednesdays but C is closed.
   3   Shops B or D: B, C and D all sell tinned goods, but C only takes cash or cheque.
   4   Shop A: A and D both sell fresh fruit and vegetables, but D doesn't open until 10 a.m.
   5   Shop D: Both A and D sell fresh fruit, but A closes at 3 p.m.

2   **1**   qualifications
      A   a degree or diploma in a relevant subject
      B   A higher qualification in mechanical engineering
      C   a degree in a relevant subject, preferably in biology or chemistry
      D   bilingual (in English and Spanish)

   2   experience
      A   five years' teaching experience
      B   previous experience of heavy goods vehicles
      C   experience in sales/marketing
      D   at least three years' relevant experience

   3   salary
      A   Send … details of current salary.
      B   (no reference to salary)
      C   The job offers an excellent salary Applications … expected salary.
      D   We offer a competitive salary …

   4   other terms of contract
      A   a one-year contract renewable
      B   (no reference to contract)
      C   (reference to 'benefits', but no details given)
      D   holiday allowance, bonus scheme and free medical insurance

   5   method of application
      A   Send CV with covering handwritten letter and details of current salary.
      B   Send career details with photograph and three professional references.
      C   Applications should include CV and mention of expected salary.
      D   For further details and an application form, phone or write to Personnel Officer Provenza SA.

pp.10–11 READING Part 2

0   **G:** *Once **this** is done, your bank manager will need to review **the plan** and discuss any overdraft facility you might need.*
this refers to the drawing up a business plan with the help of your accountant
the plan is the *business plan* referred to in the previous sentence

8   **D:** *For example, you might be in a less prosperous region where **grants** are made to encourage the start-up of small businesses.*
For example refers to an example of being entitled to *government subsidies or similar financial help.*
grants these are examples of *government subsidies* referred to in the previous sentence

9   **E:** *You may be due a repayment of income tax deducted **while you were in employment**, so do this as soon as possible.*
This refers to the previous sentence (*tell the Inland Revenue that) you have left your job.*

10   **B:** *Even if your sales are under **that figure**, it may be worthwhile registering voluntarily because you could recover what you have been charged on your business purchases.*
that figure refers to *a certain amount* in the previous sentence. VAT stands for Value Added Tax referred to in the previous sentence.

11   **A:** *It is a good idea, when considering **this issue**, to ask your local Fire Authority to check your work premises in order to ensure that they comply with current fire regulations.*
this issue is the issue of Health and Safety, referred to in the previous sentence. Fire regulations are, of course, about safety, e.g. preventing fire or the spread of fire, ensuring escape routes in the event of fire, etc.

12 F: *If **this** includes a commitment to employ **disabled people**, you will need to ensure that your premises are equipped to accommodate them, for example with ramps for wheelchairs, special provision of toilets, and so on.*
this refers to *equal opportunity* in the previous sentence
disabled people are one category, like women, ethnic minorities and old people, who do not always have equal opportunity

Choice C: *If you are new to this, talk to your local Chamber of Commerce about placing suitable advertisements in the local press.*
There is no place in the text where this sentence would fit.

pp.12–13 READING Part 3

13 A: *since it takes the pressure off them* (lines 14–15), i.e. the pressure to solve problems
B/C: The words *you, as leader, the top person with the top salary, have the sole responsibility and the know-how to solve every single problem yourself* (lines 9–12) are what the boss thinks about her/himself, not what the staff necessarily think.
D: The words *and it satisfies their natural urge to leave the solving of problems to others* (lines 15–16) do not mean that the problems were necessarily caused by others.

14 B: *A series of one-to-one meetings* (line 25)
A: The text says that you should ask them about their problems (lines 30–33).
C: This is something that will be done later, but not at the first meeting.
D: The text specifies that the first meetings should be with each person separately.

15 C: *Overlap in their responses is a useful pointer to the priorities needing your attention.* (lines 42–44)
A: No overlap means a *disunited group* (line 46), so overlap means the group works well together.
B: If no clear picture emerges, i.e. you don't get the same answers from different people, it means *that your people are part of the problem* (line 49).
D: The department may be working well, but there is nothing in the text about the number of serious problems there might be.

16 D: *Compare the views of your department with this external viewpoint* (lines 53–54)
A: The text advises you to be *open to criticizm and to praise* (lines 52–53), but does not specify that customers are likely to be more honest and open.
B: A good boss will do this, but it is not specifically mentioned in the text.
C: The text says that it is the customers, not you, who will criticize or praise (lines 51–54).

17 A: *the analysis will reveal how many and what kind of staff your company really needs* (lines 66–67)
B: This is too vague to be a good answer.
C: *There will be some grumbling that the new figures*

involve extra work (lines 64–65), but this not something that you *learn from the analysis*.
D: This may be true but the text does not specifically mention this.

18 C: *This will prompt useful discussion* (line 79)
A: It is not just the graph, but the whole discussion that will do these things.
B: The text says *tell them about your research findings* (lines 72–73); the graph is only a part of the feedback.
D: This may well happen at a later stage, but it is not specifically mentioned in the text.

FURTHER PRACTICE AND GUIDANCE (pp.14–15)

1 1 Both: see lines 35–39.
   2 It means that you can easily identify the main problems requiring your attention (see lines 42–44).
   3 It means that they do not work as a united team (see lines 44–46).
   4 It means that the people are part of the problem (see lines 48–49).
   5 Customers (line 52); and financial information (lines 57–58).

2 1 If your staff can encourage you to do all the problem-solving, it means that they don't have to do it.
   2 There are just two people in the interview: one is the interviewer, the other is the interviewee.
   3 The word *their* refers to the employees. If several of them say the same thing (i.e. their views overlap), it highlights the most important issues.
   4 The gap is the difference between your employees' view and your customers' view of the situation. Where there is a big difference, you know you have a problem.
   5 It will tell you a) if you have more people than you need to do any particular job and b) if the employee is overpaid in relation to his/her skill level (see lines 66–67).
   6 The word *this* refers to the action of providing a graph as a basis for discussion (see line 75). The graph is designed to prompt discussion, i.e. get people talking.

3 1 something that needs to be dealt with
   2 you and nobody else is responsible
   3 the expertise, the necessary knowledge and skills
   4 this is what they instinctively want to do
   5 do this (use existing resources) to see if it will solve your problem
   6 the situation as it is now
   7 sort out, deal with
   8 it will take a lot of time to do this

9 gather the information that will help you to understand better what is happening
10 the things that worry them, but which may not worry other people
11 tell them, make them realize
12 where important things are missing
13 the measures that you would normally use
14 decide which things need to be done first
15 how easy it will be to carry out your plans

pp.16–17 READING Part 4

0 B *cover* the cost
accept, e.g. a claim for expenses; *solve* a problem; *deduct* one amount from a larger amount

19 C *estimated* = made an informed guess
assessed = made an assessment of the amount; *valued* = put a price on something; *analyzed* the situation in order to make an estimate

20 A *claim* the money owing to them
ask for the money, but *ask back the money* is not possible; *demand the money*, but *demand back* is not possible; they could not *forget to require*

21 D *receipts* are evidence that you have paid *an invoice* or *bill*
you buy *tickets* for the cinema, theatre, ball game, etc.

22 A *conducted* an interview
produced a result e.g. a report; *led* a discussion; *caused* something to happen

23 D have an *attitude towards* something
an *opinion* about something; *behaviour* and *conduct* (way of behaving in a particular situation) do not fit in this context

24 C *revealed*, i.e. showed
to *expose* is to reveal something which people want to keep hidden; to *display* is to show publicly what you have found out; *discovered* would fit, but not *uncovered*

25 B *manage* = keep proper records of their expenses
run a business; *control* is possible, but it suggests that their expenses will be very high if they don't do something about them; *adopt* does not make sense in this context

26 A *trips* = i.e. travel involving short visits on business
tours and *excursions* refer to pleasure trips; *voyages* refer to travel by ship

27 D *reimbursed* expenses
(they) wait to be returned by their company does not make sense – it is the money which is returned; *reward* someone for doing something special; *recompense* someone for something they have suffered

28 D *rely* on = credit cards were the only way to pay
count on someone to help you; *call on* someone (to do something); *decide on* a course of action

29 A *supply* them with cash, i.e. give them some cash
equip = give them some kind of equipment; *involve* = include someone or something; *treat* someone with kindness, etc. or *treat* them to a meal

30 A *in advance* is a fixed expression
give them money *in case* they need it; pay a sum of money *in settlement* of a debt; *pay in arrears* is to pay for a service, etc. afterwards

31 B *hindered* they will get their money back but there are obstacles (e.g. they must produce receipts)
prevented means that they will not get their money back; *interrupted* and *obtained* do not make sense in this context

32 C *spend* (time) is a fixed expression meaning to devote an amount of time to doing something
pass and *bring* are wrong; *use (time)* means something different, e.g. use (make use of) your time wisely, don't waste it

33 C Having to use cash is an *inconvenience*, but not a *disturbance*.
You feel *embarrassment* when you have done something stupid; and *discomfort* when you are not happy with a situation or when you feel mild physical pain, e.g. a stomach-ache.

p.18 READING Part 5

0 A
research is a mass (uncountable) noun, so you cannot say *a research*, but *a piece of research*.
Compare *The cost of **paper** has gone up considerably.* and *Write your ideas on **a piece of paper**.*

00 CORRECT

34 IT
Here is how to improve your message, i.e. **This is the way** to improve ...
Confusion with *Here it is*, e.g. *Where's that list of returned goods?* **Here it is**.

35 HAVE
to speak to someone
Confusion with **to have to speak to**.

36 SO
if you **have even reached** the right person
Confusion with *even so*, e.g. *I understand why you missed the meeting.* **Even so**, *you should have let us know you weren't coming.*

37 CORRECT

38 OUT

*If you **leave an alternative number**, say it slowly ...*
Confusion with *leave out*, e.g. *Phone codes in the UK begin with 0, e.g. 01454, but if you are phoning from outside the UK, **leave out** the 0 after the international code, i.e. (0044) 1454, etc.*

39 OF

*make **sure the bleep sounds***
Confusion between *make sure that something happens* and *make sure of something*.

40 CORRECT

41 THERE

*start ... **all over again***
Confusion with *over there*, e.g. *Where's the paper? It's **over there** on the table near the window.*

42 FAR

*callers don't leave a message, **so** it may be better to*
Confusion with *so far* as in *So far, so good.* or *So far as I know, the plan still has not been approved.*

43 TOO

*it will cost you **much less** to pay*
Confusion with *too much*, e.g. *I think you paid **too much** for your car. You should have got it for much less!*

44 BUT

*a client **who is unable to***
Confusion with *a client **who tries, but is unable to** get through.*

45 CORRECT

p.19 WRITING Part 1

Sample answer

> It will cost more to repair our old printer than to buy a new one. Also, we need one which will produce better colour quality. I know that PrintMart are offering discounts at the moment, so they might be able to give us a good deal.

[46 words]

The email covers all the points:
- the reason for not repairing the old printer: *It will cost more to repair our old printer than to buy a new one.*
- what you need from a new one: *which will produce better colour quality.*
- suggestion about where to buy a new one: *PrintMart are offering discounts ... a good deal.*

FURTHER PRACTICE AND GUIDANCE (pp.20–21)

1	1F	2C	3H	4A	5C	6I	7E
	8I	9B	10F	11H	12G		

2 1 The email covers the three points (giving the reason for not repairing the old printer, saying what the new one should do, and suggesting where to buy a new one).
It is 58 words long, which is 8 words too many.
2 Sentence 1: *by* should be *buy*
Sentence 2: *product* should be *produce*
3 Sentence 2: *really good printer* should be *a really good printer*
Sentence 3: *do* should be *are doing*
Sentence 4: *I suggest to give* should be *I suggest giving/that we (should) give*
4 *Another thing* is not needed, and is too informal. *Also we really need a good ... would* be more appropriate and reduce the number of words. Avoid slang expressions like *give them a bell*. Use *phone/call them* instead.
5 The first sentence needs to be rephrased. *There's no point ... because ...* is not needed. Also, it is better to avoid repeating *repair(ing) the old printer*. These amendments will also reduce the number of words.

p.22 WRITING Part 2

Sample answer

> *Companies investigated*
>
> *I attach advertisements for two companies: Windspeed and A-to-Z. Windspeed belongs to the Freight Transport Association and A-to-Z to the Road Haulage Association.*
>
> *Services available*
>
> *A-to-Z provides a service which is essential to us, that is, the handling of hi-tech equipment.*
>
> *We shall need to hire crates for storage of equipment which our branch does not need immediately. I have checked, and A-to-Z also provide crates.*
>
> *Windspeed also does international removals, but that is not of any interest to us.*
>
> *Both companies provide a packing service, but they are quite expensive, and I suggest that we do the packing ourselves.*
>
> *Estimates*
>
> *Both companies will provide an estimate at no charge.*
>
> *Recommendation*
>
> *I recommend A-to-Z because they handle hi-tech equipment. However, we should ask both companies for an estimate so that we can compare prices.*

[137 words]

pp.23–24 LISTENING Part 1

Conversation 1

1   *A109R* (Don't confuse this with the personal reference number which is also given. The man says, 'That's my reference. It should begin with A1.' and the woman replies, 'Silly me, yes. It's A109R.')

2   *leader* (This comes in the middle of an exchange about wearing comfortable clothing. The man says, 'It's Briggs, actually. He's the course leader for the day.')

3   *(Room) 16* (The man says, 'Room 16. It's a seminar room in the West Building.')

4   *safety* (The man says, 'Also, you'll be trying out the fire-extinguishers and other safety equipment.')

Conversation 2

5   *Main Hall* (Don't be distracted by the mention of 'more than thirty'. Mark Nolan says, 'If it's more than thirty, I can offer you the Main Hall but, as I said, that will hold up to a hundred ...')

6   *extension* (The man says, 'There's the Garden Room ... in our extension ...')

7   *a lift* (The man says, '... you said you needed wheelchair access and I want to reassure you that there is a lift.')

8   *reserve places* (The man says, 'There is a big function on the same weekend so what we're thinking of doing is reserving places for your delegates.')

Conversation 3

9   *customer number* (The woman says, 'Could you confirm your customer number?' and this is followed by the number given on the form.)

10 *CPJ* Take care to get the right letters. The woman says, 'And is that order number W36936QCPF?' and the man replies, 'Almost. The last letter isn't F, it's J.')

11 *filing cabinet* (It's not a chair. The man says, 'But then it says here that I ordered a chair. It should be a filing cabinet!')

12 *nil/nothing/0/free* (The man says, 'I was told that orders over £500 are free.')

FURTHER PRACTICE AND GUIDANCE (p.25)

2   **Conversation 2**
    5   a type or name of a room
    6   a location
    7   something which is useful/essential for wheelchair users
    8   an activity

    Conversation 3
    9   a code name
   10 numbers and/or letters
   11 office furniture
   12 sum of money (reference to cost of p&p)

3   None of the gaps requires more than one word.

4   The text sections are:
    1   'Silly me, yes. It's A109R.'
    2   'It's Briggs, actually. He's the course leader for the day.'
    3   'Room 16. It's a seminar room in the West Building.'
    4   'Also you'll be trying out the fire-extinguishers and other safety equipment.'

The order of the recording does not always follow the order of the text. For example, the answer for gap 3 comes after the answer for gap 4 in the recording.

p.26 LISTENING Part 2

Section 1

13 **H** (The clues are: the woman enjoys meeting guests and she has to sort out problems with their rooms, etc.)

14 **A** (The clues are: he is in charge of organizing events, and the word 'delegate' which is the name given to people who attend conferences.)

15 **C** (The clues are: it's a job often done by men, it's an important position as the previous owner of the company filled this position, the managers answer to her and she is interested in management style, etc.)

16 **G** (The clues are: he is interested in computers, he helps people with their computer problems.)

17 **F** (The clues are: the word 'calculations' and the phrase 'make sure the books balance'.)

Section 2

18 **C** (The clues are: he is very untidy in his appearance and in his work space. He isn't, however, disorganized as he always knows where to find things.)

19 **H** (The clues are: the man is always 'having a go' at the staff and telling them what to do all the time.)

20 **E** (The clues are: she doesn't do anything, she paints her nails in the office and sits around chatting.)

21 **A** (The clues are: he can criticize but he can't explain what is wrong and he expects people to respond even when he treats them without respect. He doesn't know how to talk to staff.)

22 **B** (The clues are: he can't get to a meeting on time because he is so unpunctual.)

pp.27–28 LISTENING Part 3

23 **B**: *I actually believe that it's cheap imports that are mostly to blame.*
    A: He says it's impossible to keep the staff happy all the time.
    C: He says the marketing people *do* have good ideas sometimes.

24 A: *...if we are going to increase profits we have to look at a reduction in staff numbers in certain areas.*
B: She suggests enhancing bonus payments for increased productivity.
C: She agrees with the man that reducing overtime rates would cause a problem with the Union.

25 C:
Woman: *I'd rather run it past the Board on Tuesday. After all, the Chief Executive is going to be there.*
Man: *I agree, let's talk to them all about it then.*
A: The Union is mentioned in regard to reducing overtime rates.
B: They agree not to speak to the CE first.

26 C: *I think the most important thing is to outline what we think the company should look like, how we plan to cut down on staff, ...*
A: He says the proposed restructuring should make reference to research done so far.
B: The woman says she has been working on an economic forecast for the next five years.

27 B: *I don't think we are going to get a good response from the staff when they hear about job losses.*
A: She says she doesn't expect the staff to understand that the company's position is so serious.
C: The man thinks that most of the staff will eventually accept the new conditions.

28 C: *... perhaps you could sort of suggest how useful you could be in seeing it all through ... I can see you as the director of operations!*
A: She suggests ironically that Alain would be happy for her to accept redundancy.
B: She suggests ironically that Alain thinks she ought to ask for a big pay rise.

29 B: *I don't think you're being serious, Alain. This is much too risky to laugh about.*
A: The man says that she should trust him not to leave the company at the moment.
C: She says she doesn't understand how Alain could leave the company at the moment.

30 A: *We need to do some more thinking.*
B: She says they will need something more concrete (specific) by the end of the week.
C: He says they aren't ready to write anything down yet.

SPEAKING

FURTHER PRACTICE AND GUIDANCE (pp.30–31)

1 1D   2E   3J   4F   5C   6I   7L
       8H   9A

2 1C   2F   3J   4B   5I   6E   7K
       8H   9D   10G   11L   12A

3 Exercise 1   1B   2G   3K
       Exercise 2   1 4   2 7   3 10

4 1 (answer) I don't enjoy taking exams very much.
          (extended response) I just get very nervous but I love studying.
       2 (answer) My home town is Novi Sad but I'm working in Belgrade at the moment.
          (extended response) It's not a bad place but I miss my friends and family.
       3 (answer) Let me see. I'm the eldest of four and the only one working.
          (extended response) My two brothers and my sister still live at home.

TEST TWO

pp.34–35 READING Part 1

0   **D** Refers to the words *This event ... broaden your business contacts.*

1   **D** Refers to the words *Admission is free.*

2   **B** Refers to the words *accommodation in twin-bedded rooms.*

3   **C** Refers to the words *managing staff.*

4   **C** Refers to the words *and above all to demonstrate ways of developing their careers.*

5   **A** Refers to the words *machine translation and interpreter skills.*

6   **A** Refers to the words *specialist areas ... stocks and shares.*

7   **D** Refers to the words *planning successful conferences, trade fairs and exhibitions.*

pp.36–37 READING Part 2

0   **G**: *It is **better** to say you're from the United States.*
better refers to a comparison with what went before, i.e. better than referring to their country as 'America'.

8   **B**: *So, before opening your mouth in this country, learn to speak a few words and avoid committing a cultural offence.*
So means *in view of what has just been said*, i.e. *that Brazilians have a Portuguese heritage and speak Portuguese*
in **this** country refers to Brazil

9   **D**: *However, when scheduling meetings in São Paulo, you'll find business settings just the opposite: quite formal.*
However signals that a contrast or contradiction is about to be made. The contrast is between the habits of Rio (*a somewhat casual environment*) and São Paulo (*just the opposite*).

10 **A**: *In Rio, **on the other hand**, your host may not always be so punctual.*
Another contrast between São Paulo (*lateness is considered rude*) and Rio (*may not always be so punctual*).

11 **F**: *Soon after **this formality**, the title is usually dropped at the request of your host.*
this formality refers to the previous sentence *Formalize ...*
the title refers to preceding it with *Senhor, Senhora* or *Senhorita*

12 **C**: *This is a very impolite gesture in Brazil and likely to cause great offence.*

This refers to *the OK sign of a ring formed by the thumb and index finger* in the previous sentence, and you are advised not to use it in Brazil.

Choice E: *Good manners and polite behaviour are highly valued in business dealings in Brazil.* This may be true, but it does not fit anywhere in the text.

FURTHER PRACTICE AND GUIDANCE (pp.38–39)

1 **1** It is offensive for people from the USA to call their country *America*, because it suggests that Brazilians (and all the other peoples who live in Central and South America) are not Americans.
    2 Brazilians are proud of their Portuguese heritage and the official language of Brazil is Portuguese, not Spanish.
    3 An environment where people don't make a special effort to dress or behave in a formal manner.
    4 The writer's advice is not to let it bother you, and certainly not to make any reference or complaint about it.
    5 It starts with handshakes, an exchange of business cards and introductions.
    6 Making an upward movement with the thumb and closed fist.
    7 It's a small, very strong coffee. The visitor should accept it graciously. If they don't like it, the writer's advice is to sip it slowly.

2 **1** The word *their* refers back to North Americans.
    2 *After all* means something like *when you take all the facts into account*, and explains why Brazilians find North Americans arrogant when they refer to back home as 'America'.
    3 The word *so* links a fact (Brazilians speak Portuguese) to a consequence (to call them Spanish-Americans is insulting).
    4 *On the same note*, i.e. in the same way that North Americans forget that Brazilians also live in America, people often assume that Brazil's official language is Spanish.
    5 *At that time*, means *at the time of the first business meeting*.
    6 *Instead*, i.e. instead of using the ring sign.
    7 The word *it* refers back to the strong cup of coffee.

3 **A** He is comparing how attitudes to punctuality differ between Rio and São Paulo.
    B It refers back to the fact that Portuguese, not Spanish, is the official language of Brazil.
    C It refers to the ring sign made with thumb and forefinger.
    D *However* is similar to *on the other hand* and makes a comparison between customs in the two cities.
    São Paulo is different from Rio, because of the differing degree of formality.

E There is no linking device, which indicates that this might be the extra sentence!

F The formal way of making introductions using titles such as *Senhor*, etc, with the first name.

G It is better to use the expression *United States* rather than *America*.

4 **1 D**
It will take us all day to finish this report, <u>so</u> the boss will have to wait till tomorrow for <u>it</u>.

2 E
Labour costs in this country are very high. <u>That's why</u> the company is relocating to Karachi.

3 A
Most people use word processors these days, <u>but</u> a few still <u>prefer</u> to use pen and paper.

4 C
The reps enjoy visiting the Far East on business. <u>On the other hand, they</u> wouldn't like to live there.

5 B
Unlike most people, I enjoy writing reports. <u>I</u> just wish <u>they</u> didn't have to be done so quickly.

5

1	arrogance	13	difference
2	proud	14	different
3	late	15	indication
4	rudeness	16	indicative
5	importance	17	introduce
6	reference	18	introductory
7	arrive	19	expectation
8	approve	20	expectant
9	offer	21	offence
10	acceptance	22	offensive
11	interpretation	23	insult
12	pronounce	24	insult

pp.40–41 READING Part 3

13 **D**: *why your customer will prefer to buy your product or service rather than someone else's* (lines 8–10), i.e. why your company is more attractive than others.
A: This does not make sense. It is the customer that has market needs, and the company responds to those needs.
B: This may be true but it is not in the text.
C: This option is partly true, but it is not as precise as D, i.e. it does not say what kind of image or what the image is designed to do. Also the word *different* is meaningless in this context.

14 **A**: *The trouble is, as more and more are invented, they lose their impact.* (lines 29–30)
B: *Some people* believe this (line 23), but it is not necessarily the writer's opinion.
C/D: There is nothing in the text to support these statements.

15 **B**: *they have an honest no-nonsense ring to them.* (lines 35–36) and *projects ... image that makes the customer feel comfortable* (lines 38–39)
A: There is some truth in this *which just say what your company is about* (lines 33–34), but the writer does not specify that simple names accurately describe the product.
C: It is true that personal names are effective, but not all simple names are personal names.
D: Names that are misspelled are *eye-catching* and perhaps for that reason *easy to remember*, but the writer does not say this about personal names.

16 **C**: Lines 44–50 show that the writer thinks it is better to focus on the solution rather than on the problem because this reassures the customer.
A: This is true, but the name is negative, and the writer prefers positive names.
B: This option gives the writer's preference, but for the wrong reason.
D: There is nothing in the text to support this.

17 **A**: The writer's advice is *to ensure that the first letter of your name appears early in the alphabet* (lines 63–65)
B: The writer quotes the Finnish example, Quello, but he is talking about initial letters, not simply that your name should have an unusual letter in it somewhere.
C: This will make your name sound better (lines 56–58), but will not necessarily make it stand out.
D: This may be true, but there is nothing in the text which directly supports this.

18 **D**: *avoid the trap of choosing a name that means something offensive in another language* (lines 73–75)
A: The text says *a good translation agency will help you* (lines 72–73) but there is nothing about you providing translations.
B/C: These may be true, but there is nothing in the text to support them.

pp.42–43 READING Part 4

0 **A**: The project will *give* the companies a foothold.
make suggests the project will do more than provide the money for the companies to do something for themselves
bring suggests that the foothold already exists somewhere else
earn does not fit

19 **D**: The purpose of the project is to make the label better known abroad. Therefore it is a *campaign*, not an *event* or an *advertisement* (although these may form part of the campaign). It is not a *function* of government, i.e. it is not one of the regular jobs that governments do.

20 **A**: *launch* a boat, spaceship, campaign
fire a rocket; *pronounce* a word; *engage* doesn't make sense

21 **B:** all the words fit here, but only **promote** makes sense in the context: the companies want to *promote* brands that already exist, not to *invent*, *support* or *develop* them

22 **A:** The scheme will have **benefits** (e.g. increased sales, increased awareness of the Honduran label). The companies have *assets* and they hope they will make *profits* and pay out *dividends* to their shareholders.

23 **C:** The scheme will be **effective** if it does what it is supposed to do.
The other words don't make sense in this context: Critics *definitely* believe that only the big companies will benefit. Critics are *certain* that the scheme will only be effective if more money is put into it. Even small companies are *capable* of making some improvements to their profitability.

24 **C:** an **amount** of money
the *addition* of more money to an existing amount; the *quantity* (number) of, e.g. banknotes; the *size* of the figure

25 **D:** The **resources** needed for a successful campaign are, e.g. money, people and time.
properties would refer to buildings; *stocks*, as in stocks and shares, or quantities of goods in store; *qualities* does not make sense in this context

26 **A:** **closed** contrasts with *opened* later in the sentence
shut is similar but suggests deliberately preventing foreign investment, and requires the preposition *against*, not *to*; access is *denied*; requests are *refused*

27 **C:** The government **introduced** reforms: it *provided* the resources for companies to implement the reforms.
presented and *discovered* do not make sense in this context

28 **D:** The campaign has **attracted** investment and foreign companies have been *persuaded* to invest – the idea of investing in Honduras has appealed to them (i.e. they have found it attractive); *catch* occurs in the expression *the advertisement caught my eye*, i.e. *attracted my attention*; *claimed* does not make sense in this context

29 **A:** the text lists several **products** (textiles, etc.)
types or kinds of product; some products have *makes* or *names*, e.g. Nike trainers

30 **B:** **reached** the top
obtained (won) a prize; *performed* well; *brought* does not make sense in this context

31 **B:** make an **attempt** = try to do something
The other words do not make sense in this context.

32 **D:** the government **insists**, i.e. says very firmly
define a word (i.e. say what it means); *reserve* a place (i.e. book in advance); *presume* = suppose something to be true

33 **C:** **capable** of making an impact, i.e. will have the necessary qualities
confident of success; *worthy* of attention; *aware* of something that is happening

FURTHER PRACTICE AND GUIDANCE (pp.44–45)

1 **1** To give Honduran companies a larger share in world markets.
   2 This is the first time the government has done anything like this.
   3 They doubt it will be successful.
   4 There wasn't any until about five years ago. Now, because of government reforms, over $20 billion has been invested.
   5 Clothing, textiles, bananas and coffee do well.
   6 They must be of international quality.

2 **1** 1B   2A   3D   4C
   2 1A   2D   3B   4C
   3 1D   2B   3A   4C
   4 1A   2D   3C   4B
   5 1B   2C   3D   4A

p.46 READING Part 5

0 **CORRECT**

00 **BEEN**
Confusion between active **has continued** *to grow* and passive as in *The service* **has been discontinued**.

34 **WHO**
The reason for this is that **computers have** *printers attached to them.*
Also, *who* refers to people, *which* to things, e.g. *Computers which (or that) have printers attached to them can be very slow.*

35 **TO**
While the younger generation **are comfortable working** *on screen …*
The only preposition that could follow *comfortable* is *with*, e.g. *I am not* **comfortable with** *the way company policy is changing.*

36 **WAS**
Confusion between *there* **used to be** *a good reason* and *there* **was** *a good reason*.

37 **CORRECT**

38 **IT**
screen previews of **what was to be printed**
Compare: *I didn't know what was to happen next.* with *I never knew what it was to be happy till I met you.*

39 **CORRECT**

40 THEY
*Word processing **programs today are** capable of ...*
they would refer back to an earlier noun phrase,
e.g. *I don't like **big dogs**. **They** are capable of attacking*
without warning.

41 MANY
***so that** hard-copy drafts are ... not required*
so that here means with the result that. Confusion
with *so many*, e.g. *There are **so many** mistakes in this*
*report **that** you will need to retype the whole thing.*

42 OF
***Despite this**, people still want ...* Confusion with *in*
spite of, e.g. *In spite of this, people still want ...*

43 CORRECT

44 EVERY
***because print cartridges** and paper are both very*
expensive
Confusion with ***every** print cartridge is very*
expensive. Also, *every* would not go with the mass
noun *paper*.

45 MORE
***a much better way** of storing data*
To make a comparison, either add *-er* to the
adjective, e.g. *quick-quicker*, or put *more* before the
adjective, e.g. *common-more common*. You cannot
add both, i.e. ~~more commoner~~ is wrong.

p.47 WRITING Part 1

Sample answer

I need training in how to use our new Saga
accounting software. The local business college
organizes short courses on accounting software.
There is one next month that deals with the Saga
program. The cost is very reasonable, so I hope
you will give me permission to attend.

[48 words]

The memo covers all the points:
- what you need: *training in how to use our new Saga accounting software*
- a suitable course: *one next month that deals with the Saga program*
- asking permission: *I hope you will give me permission to attend the course.*

p.48 WRITING Part 2

Sample answer

Note: Subheadings will make your text easier for the
reader. It is also a way of making sure that you cover
all the points.

Thank you for your letter of xxxx. I am sorry that
you were dissatisfied. Please accept the following
explanations.

1 Technical support
Our regular technician was ill and we had to replace
her at very short notice. I understand that the only
problem you had was a short delay to an AV
presentation while a fuse was replaced.

2 Food
Apart from Tuesday, when there was a power cut, I
cannot understand what went wrong. I have ordered
an investigation.

3 Rates
You are absolutely right. You were invoiced at the
peak rate. I have arranged for an immediate refund
of the difference.

4 Website
Our Web Host assures me that there is no problem.
This error message can occur when there is heavy
traffic on the Internet.

Once again, I am sorry that you were unhappy with
our service.

[140 words]

FURTHER PRACTICE AND GUIDANCE (p.49)

1   *Suggested answers*
 1   I apologize if the technician had little
     experience of Powerpoint presentations.
     Unfortunately our regular technician was ill.
     (We have only just acquired Powerpoint and
     all our technicians are going on a proper
     training course next week.)
 2   I have checked the microphone concerned
     and agree it does not work properly and
     needs replacing. (The problem was solved
     once the volume was turned up.)
 3   I have spoken to the person concerned and
     the misunderstanding has now been
     resolved. (Unfortunately, the wrong rate had
     been entered in the computer at the time of
     booking.)
 4   I have checked with our host server, and I am
     assured that yours was an isolated incident.
 5   (We agree that most people would prefer
     fresh vegetables to frozen vegetables.) We
     always try to provide fresh vegetables in
     season, but otherwise we use good quality
     frozen produce.

6 I apologize if there were problems and would like to assure you that the person concerned no longer works here. (Generally however, we find that most people quickly get used to the various foreign accents, and indeed quite like having staff from other countries to serve them.)

2 Thank you for your letter. I am sorry that you were dissatisfied. Please accept the following explanations.
Our regular technician was ill, so the janitor, who is not very experienced, had to deal with the problem you had with the projector screen. As to the food, apart from Tuesday when there was a brief power cut, I do not know of any other problems in the kitchen.
With regard to your bill, you are absolutely right: you were invoiced at the peak rate. I have arranged for a refund, and can only apologize for the oversight.
Despite your difficulty in accessing our website, I am assured that there is not usually a problem, although the error message you got often occurs when the Internet is busy. I can assure you that our website functions perfectly well. Once again I apologize for our service where it was not up to your expectations.

pp.50–51 LISTENING Part 1

Conversation 1

1 *Greenhalgh* You must spell this correctly to gain a mark as it is spelled out in the text.

2 *factory*: don't confuse with the location for the meeting (The man says, 'Is that the meeting at two thirty in the afternoon at the operations building?' and the woman replies, 'I think it's at four. To discuss the plans for the new factory.')

3 *Wednesday* Not Tuesday as the woman requests to begin with. (The man says, 'Possible, but Wednesday at eleven is better.')

4 *Health and Safety* (The woman says, 'Could you ask him to bring the stuff on Health and Safety he's had approved?')

Conversation 2

5 *three PCs* (The man says, 'No. It seems that they're missing at least three PCs and they only received four printers.')

6 *next week* (The man says, 'Apparently we rang them to say the delivery was delayed until next week but it got there yesterday after all …')

7 *pay/offer compensation*
(The woman says, 'What a mess. Are they asking for compensation?' and the man replies, 'Yes. They want us to make them an offer …')

8 *extra staff* (The man says, '… to cover the extra staff they had to bring in.')

Conversation 3

9 *Sales Division* (It's for a data input clerk in the Marketing Division … no, sorry, the Sales Division, isn't it?)

10 *flexitime* (Well, what I want to know is if you do flexitime.)

11 *rate* (I've done this before so would I get the £9.40 an hour? The lower rate, that's the £6.40, wouldn't really be enough.)

12 *tomorrow/tomorrow morning/in the morning* (I'll ring again in the morning.)

p.52 LISTENING Part 2

Section 1

13 **F** (The clues are: finding out someone's interests in advance, and taking a guest out for an evening.)

14 **H** (The clues are: wearing appropriate clothes, preparing yourself well, shaking hands and answering questions.)

15 **B** (The clues are: the person you are calling cannot see you so you need to speak slowly and clearly.)

16 **C** (The clues are: it has a specific purpose, a 'main body' and an introduction and recommendations.)

17 **D** (The clues are: to write in short form, e.g. incomplete sentences, to use abbreviations and dashes.)

Section 2

18 **B** (The clues are: the staff are new to their jobs and are taking longer to understand their responsibilities. They need training.)

19 **F** (The clues are: that this is a senior position for which it will be hard to find a replacement and that he has to resign the role after a stipulated six years.)

20 **E** (The clues are: that people are not keen to invest their money in the stock market and by implication in the company's shares.)

21 **G** (The clues are: the need to investigate the quality of the suppliers.)

22 **D** (The clues are: the workforce is having difficulty coming in for early and late shifts.)

FURTHER PRACTICE AND GUIDANCE (pp.53–54)

1 1 five
   2 what each speaker is giving advice about
   3 eight (A–H)
   4 No, you can't.

2 1 F
   2 C
   3 H
   4 B

3 1 interests
2 evening
3 wonderful
4 tired
5 going
6 prefer
7 early
8 travelling

4 *Suggested answers*
… find out in advance what their interests
are./evening out/getting dressed up/going
somewhere posh/They might just prefer …/
… they could have been travelling for hours.

5 Similar language used. Both recordings talk
about how to write something.

6 **Writing a report**: check the grammar,
spelling/who is it for, why do they want it/try
reading it aloud to someone/leave the
introduction until later/what is the primary
purpose

Making notes: remember to use
abbreviations/it's not a good idea to use
complete sentences/use lots of space/remember
to use the dash/try putting in words like
because, therefore, but or *as*

pp.55–56 LISTENING Part 3

23 A
She says, '… *but what I'm really pleased about is how
I'm getting to know my customers better.*'
B: The interviewer says she markets her products
to people all over the world.
C: She has been told that the website will save her
a lot of money in postage and brochures but she
says that she will find that out in the future.

24 B
She says, '*The first decision you must take is whether
to sell over the Internet or not.*'
A: She uses feedback from her customers to make
her products more successful.
C: She thinks that this is a decision to take later on
in the design process.

25 A
She says, '… *more importantly for everyone, make sure
you give sufficient resources to the process.*'
B: You don't have to do this, but it is an option.
C: She thinks this is a good way to encourage
people to visit your site. It's not a necessity.

26 C
She says, '*I've found the surest way to get more hits –
that's people visiting your site – is to get your name
listed on other sites.*'
A: This is an option when you are developing your
site.
B: She says this is standard practice but she thinks
there are better ways.

27 C
She says, '*In fact, I closed my shop down last week and
just work from my own office at home.*'
A: She says she has always felt at home with the
technology.
B: She already knew that she would be able to
introduce products more rapidly.

28 B
She says, '*If I were to do it all again, I'd employ
someone to add new material and so on.*'
A: She says they don't really need good IT skills.
C: She says she does respond but she doesn't say
how quickly and she doesn't link this to managing
the website.

29 C
She says, '*Since I've had the website, it's more like
30%.*'
A: She hopes that the business will increase by
another 10% next year.
B: Before the introduction of the website the
business was growing by 13% a year.

30 C
She says, '*I need some quality thinking time.*'
A: She says she is not ready to start up a new
business yet.
B: She has already installed broadband.

SPEAKING

**FURTHER PRACTICE AND GUIDANCE
(pp.59–60)**

2 1b   2f   3e   4c   5a   6d

3 B: 1b   2c   3a
C: 1b   2a   3c

4 A: 1, 3, 8
B: 2, 4, 6
C: 5, 7, 9

5 1B   2D   3A   4C   5H   6E   7I   8G
9F

TEST THREE

pp.62–63 READING Part 1

0   **B**   Refers to the words *we carry out an audit to determine what skills already exist in the company.*

1   **D**   Refers to the words *at our Tutorial Centre, or, for your convenience, at your own premises.*

2   **D**   Refers to the words *getting by* which mean *just enough to survive*, e.g. to order a meal, tell a taxi driver where you want to go, etc.

3   **B**   Refers to the words *The outcome is a clear picture of training needs that allows you to invest in key training areas …*

4   **C**   Refers to the words *top-class training in making both live and written presentations.*

5   **B**   Refers to the words *there's a lot of unused talent in your company* and *aptitude tests to measure individual potential.*

6   **A**   Refers to the words *courses also available for reading technical documents.*

7   **C**   Refers to the words *design your brochures … with translated versions if you need them.*

pp.64–65 READING Part 2

0   **G**: *It provides a huge market for local suppliers as well as direct employment for more than 400,000 in nearly 700 **mines**.*
It refers to *The country's mineral wealth* in the previous sentence. The key word is **mines**: minerals have to be mined.

8   **C**: *The world-class **financial sector** is supported by a sound legal framework and is highly competitive.*
The key words are **financial sector**. This refers back to *dominated by the financial services and manufacturing sectors* and forward to the next sentence *The full range of services, from commercial, merchant and retail banking to mortgage lending and insurance* … both of which have to do with finance.

9   **F**: *It is dominated by metal and engineering, which produces 60 per cent of Africa's steel and ranks among the world's best.*
It refers back to *The manufacturing sector* in the previous sentence, and forward to *Historically, manufacturing has suffered* … in the next sentence.

10   **A**: *Nevertheless, manufacturing production has soared since 2000 as a result of lower interest rates, renewed economic growth and stronger demand for exports.*
Nevertheless tells you that a contrast or contradiction is coming. In this case, it is between the weakness referred to in the previous sentence *structural weakness … reduced its competitiveness.* The sentence also refers forward to *This trend* in the following sentence, i.e. the trend to renewed economic growth.

11   **E**: *Tourism has received a **further** boost as cruise liners have been docking at South African ports in order to avoid the Suez Canal and the Middle East **trouble spots**.*
The phrase about avoiding **trouble spots** refers back to South Africa being a *safe* destination. The key word in Sentence E is a **further** boost, i.e. a further boost to Cape Town's popularity because of the cruise liners.

12   **B**: *Alien plants not only absorb three million cubic metres more water a year than normal vegetation, but they also pose a serious fire risk.*
Sentence B gives the reason for uprooting **alien plants** referred to in the previous sentence.

Choice D: *Nor has the continuing fluctuation of the US dollar against the rand helped the domestic economy.*
This sentence does not fit anywhere in the text.

pp.66–67 READING Part 3

13   **A**: Bullies *will set impossible deadlines … make mistakes* (lines 9–11).
B: The text says that a bully is *bad news for any company* (line 6), i.e. the company will suffer. The bullies do not spread bad news.
C: The text gives an example of such a person: *an ageing male manager who could not come to terms with …* (lines 28–30), but this is not a definition of a bully.
D: The text says the opposite: that bullies may be suffering from *some kind of inferiority complex* (lines 15–16).

14   **C**: *the increase is a direct result of the current business culture with its emphasis on competition and aggressive 'masculine' management styles …* (lines 20–26)
A: The text gives the example of *an ageing male manager* who couldn't get on with female staff (lines 28–30) but this is not the same as saying that age and sex differences have caused an increase in bullying.
B: People are afraid of losing their jobs (*job insecurity*, line 25), but being strict is not the same as bullying.
D: The text says *though often the people at the top don't know* (lines 7–8) which is not the same as ignoring the situation.

15   **A**: The clue is in the sentence: *The oppressive atmosphere … spirits falling.* (lines 33–37)
B: This is true *did the wise thing and got rid of him* (lines 39–40), but this does not describe the effect the bully had on the company.

C: This is true *It wasn't easy for the staff to report him* (lines 37–38), but this does not answer the question.

D: It is true that he *could not come to terms with women in management positions* (lines 29–30), but this does not describe his effect on the company.

16 B: *employers must ensure that both sides have the opportunity to make their case* (lines 44–46)

A: It is the bully, not the victim, who is dismissed and can then appeal.

C: The writer is saying that there must be proper procedures, not just dismissal on *suspicion* of bullying.

D: This may be true but it does not define the procedure.

17 B: Collect evidence as follows: *Make a note of conversations, keep memos and letters, as these will be needed as evidence to back up your case.* (lines 61–64)

A: The writer advises you to fight back, but not in this way: *keep cool, be patient* (line 58)

C: The text says *Talk to colleagues* (line 60), but does not specify that you should persuade them to support you.

D: The writer's advice is to *be patient and take action when you are sure you can be effective* and take time to gather evidence (lines 59–60), i.e. not to do anything *immediately*.

18 D: The word *defuse* usually refers to removing the fuse from a bomb, i.e. to make it safe and remove the threat of an explosion. Here, the writer says that *Bullies don't always realize that their behaviour is offensive* (lines 64–65), and suggests that telling them about their behaviour might make them change.

A: *a few well-chosen words* are the words you use to point out diplomatically to a bully that his/her behaviour is unacceptable.

B: Telling the employer, diplomatically or not, may become necessary, but the writer is talking about bullies who might be persuaded to change their behaviour once they realize they are being offensive.

C: This is something that would only apply once the managers have been informed about a bully. It has nothing to do with the writer's point about *a few well-chosen words ... situation.*

FURTHER PRACTICE AND GUIDANCE (pp.68–69)

Exam Information

a) The text does not say that bullies believe they are better than everyone else. Bullies may have an inferiority complex, which means they think they are not as good as everyone else. And people who DO think they are superior are not necessarily bullies.

b) It means that it is a problem for the company because of the effect it has on staff morale, and can perhaps damage the company's reputation.

c) A bully sets impossible deadlines, makes fun of people and ridicules others when they make mistakes. He or she may also shout and be abusive. The bully's purpose is to make other people feel bad.

A Detailed Study

1 1   set impossible deadlines (line 9)
2   job insecurity (line 25)
3   could not come to terms with (line 29)
4   a belief in yourself and your abilities
5   a way of deciding if a person is guilty
6   make a case (line 46)
7   saying things which are designed to warn or frighten another person

2

	V	N	A
1	ignore	ignorance	ignorant
2	insult	insult	insulting
3	abuse	abuse	abusive
4	emphasise	emphasis	emphatic
5	compete	competition	competitive
6	create	creation/creature	creative
7	oppress	oppression	oppressive
8	confide	confidence	confident/confidential
9	recognize	recognition	recognizable
10	act	action	active
11	encourage	encouragement	encouraging
12	choose	choice	chosen
13	intervene	intervention	intervening
14	dismiss	dismissal	dismissive
15	persist	persistence	persistent

3   1G   2D   3A   4C   5F   6I   7B   8J
     9E   10H

pp.70–71 READING Part 4

0   A
in difficulties is a fixed expression, similar to *in trouble*

19   A
boom, (opposite: *slump, recession*): the time when a country's economy is doing well
profit (opposite: *loss*): you make a profit from the plus difference between cost and selling price
increase (opposite: *decrease*): an increase in sales should make everyone happy
The *value* of a service/product is what something is worth, e.g. *He knows the price of everything and the value of nothing.*

20   C
fashions, etc. come and *go*; living things *die* (eventually); sales *fall*; heavy objects *sink* in water

21 B

an *estimate* is a systematic or scientific *guess*; a *forewarning* refers to a guess that something bad is going to happen; people who have *insight* are aware of the real nature of a situation

22 D

we *reach* limits and targets; we *expect* something to happen, (i.e. that they will reach their spending limits); we *catch* balls, trains, etc.; we *touch* things with our fingers, or people's hearts with our words

23 B

to need something **urgently** is to need it immediately / as soon as possible; we *eagerly* look forward to something nice; we *certainly* know who we are; *hopefully* (= we hope that) we will get what we need

24 C

The phrase is *a battle … is developing*. You could only use *expanding* if there was an early reference to the battle, e.g. *A battle has begun, and it is expanding into all sectors of the economy*. Armies *arrive* on the battlefield, and the soldiers are the ones who *fight*.

25 B

profit margins is a fixed expression
The *margin* is the difference between revenue and costs: the lower the costs, the higher your profit margin. We talk about *amounts* of money, we make business *deals*, and we prefer profits to *losses*.

26 D

likely is the only one that fits in this pattern: *It is the company most likely to survive*. The others require a different pattern: *It is sure/expected to survive*; *It is probable that it will survive*.

27 D

benefit is the only option that makes sense here: the company's decision to penetrate new markets is a good decision, so it will benefit.
We *escape* from danger; we *recover* from a recession or an illness; we *emerge* from a confined space, e.g. from a difficult business meeting.

28 B

restrict is the only word that fits the meaning
They *restrict* (limit or confine) themselves, i.e. they do not open up business in minor cities.
The police use handcuffs to *restrain* a dangerous criminal. A report may *contain* (have) valuable information. We give money to *support* our favourite charities.

29 C

The expression is *cope with (a difficult situation)*. Their warehouses are full, nobody is buying – it's a difficult situation, and they must cope with it.
We *correspond with* (= write to) our business partners, BUT *In Turkey KDV corresponds to* (= is the

equivalent of) *VAT in the UK*. We *compare* one thing *with* another to see the similarities and differences. Companies *compete with* one another for customers.

30 D

items here means *manufactured things to be sold*
Objects is a general word for things that we notice. *Pieces* are the parts of something, e.g. the pieces of a jigsaw puzzle. *Substances* are materials, often chemical.

31 C

oversupply, i.e. supply exceeds demand
overload relates to an excessive demand on a power source; *overflow* refers literally to liquids; *overrun* refers to something which exceeds the time allowed for it

32 A

When times are hard, we try to *reduce* (bring down) our overheads. We can never *remove* (i.e. get rid of) them completely. We *adapt* to changed circumstances. We *adjust* (i.e. make small changes), so we could try adjusting costs and work practices in order to reduce our overheads.

33 B

The strategy is *working*, (i.e. it is successful) so the manufacturers are *winning* the battle. The text tells us what is *happening* in general, and some of the (unexpected) things that *occur*.

p.72 READING Part 5

0   CORRECT

00 IF

a new airport lounge as part of a £1.7m renovation
Read the whole sentence and you see that there is no *if*-clause.

34 ON

the new lounge will offer
Confusion with *on offer*, e.g. *A lot of goods are on offer in the sale*.

35 CORRECT

36 TO

the new changes mean … users will also benefit
Possible confusion with *The airport says the new changes are going to mean …*

37 CORRECT

38 BE

The renovation … will involve
Confusion with the passive *will be involved*, e.g. *How many people will be involved in the work?*

39 WHICH

an increase … from eight to twelve, including two desks for ticket holders
Possible confusion with *an increase … from eight to twelve, which includes two desks*.

40 MUCH
with more shops
Confusion between *much* (singular) and *many* (plural): *with many more shops* would be correct. Compare with *with much more space.*

41 CORRECT

42 ITS
of Norwich Airport
Possible confusion with *Norwich and its airport,* which still wouldn't make sense.

43 BY
over the next ten years = in or during the next ten years
Confusion with *by (the end) of the period,* e.g. *by the year 2020.*

44 IT
work ... is expected to be completed
The question form *is it expected* does not make sense. The question would be something like *Is the work expected to be completed ...?*

45 NO
in time for the summer season
in time for is a fixed expression
Confusion with *in no time* = very quickly, e.g. *If we all join in, the job will be finished in no time.*

FURTHER PRACTICE AND GUIDANCE (p.73)

1 1 *of*: Compare: *because of (something)* and *because it was a.*
   2 *for*: Compare: *go out for a breath* and *go out to get a breath.*
   3 *to*: Compare: *(I want you) to make sure* and *please make sure.*
   4 *not*: Compare: *Why don't you open* and *Why not open.*
   5 *as*: Compare: *are well up* and *(X) as well as (Y),* e.g. *We have made money on sales as well as on rentals.*
   6 *been*: Compare: *was forced* and *has been forced.*
   7 *that*: Compare: *twelve people including the janitor* and *twelve people. That includes the janitor.*
   8 *so*: Compare: *they gave me time off, so I was very grateful* and *they gave me time off, for which I was very grateful.*
   9 *me*: Compare: *looked up at me* and *looked up.* There is a phrasal verb *look something up* which means to check the meaning of something. If you *look somebody up,* you go and visit somebody you know.
   10 *then*: Compare: *since then* (*We saw him a month ago, and we haven't seen him since then.*) and *since we last saw him.*

2 1 False. The business lounge is only part of the renovation.
   2 True. (The text says, '... a new airport lounge ... part of a £1.7m renovation of the terminal building ...'.)
   3 False. It is also a place where business travellers can work.
   4 False. The transit service will be improved.
   5 True, as a result of increasing the number of check-in desks.
   6 True. (The text says, '... including two desks for ticket holders with carry-on luggage only.')
   7 True. (The text says, '... more shops ...')
   8 True. (The text says, 'With passenger figures expected to double over the next ten years ...'.)
   9 False. (The text says, 'Work ... to be completed by May ...')

p.74 WRITING Part 1

Sample answer

> We need to find ways to reduce the cost of using office phones. Please make your calls brief, and use alternative methods of communication, e.g. email or fax, especially for overseas messages. You may not use office phones for private calls except in an emergency.

[45 words]

The memo covers all the points:
- the situation: *cut down the cost of using office phones*
- how to save money: *make your calls brief, and use alternative methods ... especially for overseas messages*
- private use of phones: *You may not use office phones ... except in an emergency.*

FURTHER PRACTICE AND GUIDANCE (pp.75–76)

1 **Instruction 1**: C E G L
   Instruction 2: A D F J
   Instruction 3: B H I K

2 1 Does it cover all points? Yes. It explains the problem (*too long on the phone ... costing the earth*). It suggests alternatives (*use email, use off-peak times*). It gives an instruction about private use of phones (no private calls, except emergencies). But it is one word over the word limit.
   2 Spelling: in the last line, *maybe* (meaning *perhaps*) should be written as one word. Punctuation: the comma in *Some of you, spend ...* is not needed. It would be better to split the last sentence into two sentences *... for your private stuff. Well, maybe if ...*

3 and 4

Style: The memo is written in a *very* informal style with direct personal references (*Some of you ...*, *And no way should you use ...*), and several colloquial expressions (*costing the earth*, *And no way*, *personal stuff*, *get your supervisor's OK*). Office memos are usually much more formal and impersonal than this.

3 The company telephone bill for the last quarter is / **D** up by 75% over the previous quarter. An analysis of the / **C** numbers given in the detailed statement shows that several / **A** calls were made to Australia and other / **F** countries with which we do not do business. Clearly, these can only / **B** be personal calls. Any member of staff found / **E** making personal calls on company phones, other / **G** than emergency calls, will be asked to cover the cost of the calls.

p.77 WRITING Part 2

Sample answer

Tractors accounted for half the equipment bought in 2003, and soil preparation machinery for 25%. 10% of purchases were combine harvesters and 10% earth-moving equipment. Irrigation equipment like pumps and small machines make up the rest.

The period has seen a decline in British manufacturing to only 5% of market share, with many small companies going out of business. European countries are our biggest suppliers. Their market share has almost doubled in the period 1993–2003 from 35% to 60%. Many European companies now have assembly plants in the UK. The USA and Canada are our second biggest source, with their market share growing from 15% to 25%. They are the main suppliers of big machines like combine harvesters. The rest of our imports come from other countries, of which Japan accounts for 5%, supplying mostly small-scale specialist equipment.

[139 words]

The model answer contains some useful language items that you need when you are reporting data from a graph or a table, e.g.:
- making comparisons about quantities, e.g. *market share has doubled*, *biggest supplier*, *second biggest source*
- describing trends, e.g. *a decline in manufacturing*, *market share growing from ... to ...*, *going out of business*
- useful expressions, e.g. *account for*, *make up the rest*.

pp.78–79 LISTENING Part 1

Conversation 1

1 *Jarrold's* (The man says, 'It's Mike Ponti from Jarrold's speaking. That's J-A DOUBLE R-O-L-D apostrophe S.') You need to spell this correctly to gain a mark as the spelling is given.

2 *catering supplies* (Mike says, 'I ordered some stationery last week, sorry, I mean catering supplies.')

3 *JR0023* (Mike says, 'The order code is, let me see, 456Y – no that's one of the product codes. It's JR0023.')

4 *catalogue* (Mike says, 'Also, could you let me know if your new catalogue is out? I'd like a copy, please.') Don't confuse this with the price list which he hopes is in the catalogue.

Conversation 2

5 *Publicity Department* (She says, 'I'm in Marketing ... sorry, no. We call ourselves the Publicity Department now!')

6 *management course* (She says, 'But what I actually want to discuss with him is the possibility of going on a management course.') Don't confuse with the training programme the man mentions earlier.

7 *training budget* (She says, 'Well, I don't know how much is left in the training budget for our department.')

8 *branch* (She says, 'The thing is I'm heading up our West London branch in three months' time.')

Conversation 3

9 *Easy Finance* (The man says, 'I'm phoning on behalf of my company, Easy Finance Ltd.') Don't confuse this with the name of the car hire company which is ABC Car Hire.

10 *Company Car* (The woman says, 'You mean the Company Car scheme? It lets you have up to six cars on permanent loan for a minimum of six months.') Don't confuse this with the other scheme she mentions called the Premium Rate scheme.

11 *special deal* (The man says, 'Can you do us a special deal?')

12 *tomorrow afternoon* (The man says: 'In fact I'm coming your way tomorrow afternoon – or else sometime next week?') The alternative of coming next week isn't possible because the manager will be on holiday.

p.80 LISTENING Part 2

Section 1

13 **F** (The clues are: 'It's about our meeting tomorrow at eleven. I can't make it.' Note that instructions are mentioned and he isn't apologizing for cancelling the appointment.)

14 **A** (The clues are: 'Just wanted to explain why I had to leave early yesterday.' and 'Anyway, hope you understand.' You should also be able to pick up on her apologetic tone.)

15 **D** (The clues are: 'I just wanted to change something on the list I left with you.' and 'So what I'm going to need is another 24 slabs, please.' He mentions he won't complain about anything but don't confuse this with G.)

16 **G** (The clues are: 'This has caused me a lot of embarrassment, I can tell you.' You should also be able to pick up on his tone of voice.)

17 H (The clues are: 'What we do is send the customer a copy of our complaints procedure with a covering letter acknowledging their letter and saying the matter is being looked in to.' There are several words and phrases which suggest she is explaining something, for example 'Next ...' 'Then we ...')

Section 2

18 G (The clues are: 'This will be the first time I've talked to her about what I think the senior staff, including myself, need to develop our skills and so on.' and 'No, I want some good advice on what sort of courses are available on managing risk or strategic thinking.' Medical emergencies are mentioned so don't confuse this with D.)

19 D (The clues are: the secretary has been injured while moving something in the office and the visitor is coming to explain the health and safety rules to them.)

20 H (The clues are: '... it's a François Germain from Paris and it looks like he's interested in the new range that's coming out in the spring.' Research is mentioned but don't be attracted to E.)

21 B (The clues are: the meeting is about the legal implications of making staff redundant. Management consultants are mentioned so don't be attracted by A.)

22 F (The clues are: the visitor is coming to discuss job applicants and will be responsible for arranging interviews, etc. Security is mentioned so don't be attracted by C.)

pp.81–82 LISTENING Part 3

23 B: *Actually, around 70% of businesses in this country are run by families which makes them, statistically speaking, the backbone of the economy.*
A: There is no suggestion that they are more successful than other businesses.
C: The interviewer says that productivity isn't significantly different between the two types of companies.

24 B: *what is significant is that an average lifespan of nearly 22 years for a family-run business ...*
A: Staff turnover is less than 15%.
C: 70% of businesses are family-run.

25 A: *One of the warnings that business advisers give is that working long hours can put too much pressure on a relationship.*
B: They work in the same office but this isn't an issue.
C: They talk about the importance of taking time off.

26 B: *But basically, now, we both work all the hours under the sun, and we don't have a problem because we both understand the demands of the business.*
A: We don't know how old their children are now but there are still parental duties to perform.
C: They agreed to share duties when the children were very young but it didn't work out like that.

27 C: *No, what I find works best when I'm feeling really stressed is to put some music on and then I calm right down.*
A: Jill has suggested getting a dog but they haven't actually got one yet.
B: Scott likes golf but this is not what he finds most relaxing and he can't always play when he wants to.

28 B: *Sometimes we don't see eye-to-eye on artistic matters.*
A: They have an accountant so they don't disagree on financial matters.
C: Jill leaves the technical side to Scott.

29 C: *I think on a Monday morning when there's a pile of letters to answer, I could do with that sort of help!*
A: Scott says he argued more with his male colleagues.
B: Jill says she doesn't miss meals out. Scott doesn't mention it.

30 C: *Well, we want to extend our range and that means more time on the design side of the business.*
A: They are already increasing their exports.
B: They have already taken on more permanent staff.

FURTHER PRACTICE AND GUIDANCE (pp.83–84)

1 1, 3, 4, 5, 6, 8

2 1 three
   2 interviewer, Jill, Scott
   3 C (a discussion)

3 1, 3, 5, 7, 9, 10

4 See explanation in Key for questions 23–30 for Test 3.

SPEAKING

FURTHER PRACTICE AND GUIDANCE (pp.88–89)

2 1F 2H 3A 4D 5B 6C 7E 8G

3 1d 2c 3a 4e 5b 6c 7d 8a
   9e 10b

4 1 1/7 2 4/9 3 2 4 8

TEST FOUR

pp.90–91 READING Part 1

0   **D**   Refers to the words *Please enter in the log ... paper used.*

1   **A**   Refers to the words *sixty minutes for lunch.*

2   **D**   Refers to the words *In the event ... Office Manager ...*

3   **B**   Refers to the words *inform ... if any of your colleagues are absent.*

4   **C**   Refers to the words *inform your immediate superior before going to the Sick Room.*

5   **A**   Refers to the words *block times* (i.e. when all employees are in).

6   **B**   Refers to the words *Close ... building.*

7   **D**   Refers to the words *Use of the machine ... strictly forbidden.*

pp.92–93 READING Part 2

0   **G**: *Dragon Systems invented **it as far back as 1984**, and although a one-person system cost £32,000 eight years ago, there are now excellent SR software packages available for as little as £30.*
The word *it* refers back to SR development. The words *as far back as 1984* refer to *The idea is not new ...* in the previous sentence.

8   **C**: *There is a very good reason for **that moment of hesitation**: the system knows how words go together!*
that moment of hesitation refers to *the system waits a fraction of a second* in the previous sentence

9   **A**: ***This** is to see if it makes statistical sense, that is, to assess which combination of the words is most probable and how likely it is that they would appear in this context.*
This refers to what the system does, i.e. *checks the two words before it and the two words after it.*
Sentence A also refers forward to an example given in the following sentence: *For example, ...*

10   **F**: ***Now**, all the major producers have brought in ways of allowing business users to dictate to their laptop and send their words back to the office.*
The word *now* contrasts with what was the case before now, i.e. it relates to the expression *At first, ...* in the previous sentence. The contrast is between the old way – *sit in front of their desktop* – and the new way – *dictate to their laptop.*

11   **D**: ***They** can **even** cope with English spoken by Parisians, Italians or south Londoners, who all talk very fast.*
They refers to *These modern systems* in the previous sentence. A key word is *even*, which emphasises how *remarkably quickly* the systems work.

12   **E**: *What is **even more exciting** is that modern systems can now take spoken words as **commands** to the computer.*
The key words are *even more exciting*, i.e. even more exciting than the speed of modern systems described in the previous paragraph: *These modern systems not only translate your speech into screen text, but they do so remarkably quickly.* The word *commands* in Sentence E refers forward to *Virtually every instruction ...* in the next sentence.

Choice B: *And because women generally speak more clearly than men, speeds for women are even faster.* This may be true, but it doesn't fit anywhere in the text.

FURTHER PRACTICE AND GUIDANCE (pp.94–95)

1   *Suggested answers*
   1   Probably in the USA.
   2   Because for a time they sold better than the most popular computer games.
   3   Because it checks two words before and after each utterance to make sure it has understood the context.
   4   It connects with a PC and sends a spoken report into the SR program (Dragon's Naturally Speaking program).
   5   They recognize commands and act on them.
   6   You say the person's name and their address comes up automatically.

2   **A**   It refers to the way the program checks the two words preceding and following what you say.
   B   It is difficult to find a reference back or forward for this, so this is the extra sentence.
   C   The fraction of a second before the program responds.
   D   *They* refers to the modern systems that can do so much more than the earlier versions of the program. The word *even* refers back to the words *not only.*
   E   The fact that the modern SR programs can recognize words that give a command to the computer is even more exciting than the high speeds now achieved.
   F   It contrasts with the previous situation when the program was first introduced people had to sit in front of their desktops to use the SR program (i.e. the word *Now* contrasts with the words *At first*).
   G   The SR program (see the example).

3 1 That
2 They
3 worse/more serious
4 even (*also* is possible, but the exclamation mark (!) makes *even* the more likely word)
5 both
6 first(ly), second(ly)
7 Not only
Not only links to *but it can also ...*
8 because/on account/as a result
These phrases link to the following preposition *of* and introduce the explanation for why the company ran at a loss.
9 between
Between links the word *difference* to the two words to be defined (*invoice* and *bill*).
10 it
It refers back to the SR program.

4 The biggest employment advance of recent years is what so many career-minded mothers have wanted for decades: half a job. Half a real job, that is, with all the advantages, pay rises and prospects that go / **C** with a full-time career, in return for an investment of half the hours and half the responsibility. More and more companies are beginning to realize / **E** that it is better to have a good employee on her own terms than not to have her at all. Jobs can be / **G** shared in many ways: alternate weeks, mornings or afternoons. But however the scheme is organized, the most important part of the job-sharer's week is the handover period, when a job-sharer gets a crucial update / **D** from the other half of the team on all that has happened in her absence. But, however well skills and time priorities have been matched, the success of a job-share depends to a large extent / **F** on the chemistry of its sharers. If there is suspicion or jealousy instead of trust, or if their work styles vary, inconsistency may set in and efficiency will suffer. Job-sharing isn't only popular with working mothers. British Airways recently received an appeal / **B** from a childless senior computer worker who is seeking to share his job simply to improve his quality of life. The computer worker explained that he and his wife had both been working for years and felt there was not much sense in / **A** accumulating a lot of money when there are things they would both much rather be doing.

pp.96–97 READING Part 3

13 **A**: *requires a much smaller initial investment* (lines 5–6)
B: A manufacturer is more aware of what its customers want (lines 17–19). Service sector start-ups are more *speculative* (line 21).
C: We are not told if a service business has difficulty finding trained staff.
D: This is true (line 8), but this is not why a service business is easier to start up.

14 **D**: *so payback may be seriously delayed* (lines 22–23)
A: They may incur promotional costs (lines 13–14), but the text does not say that they must do this.
B: The text refers to the fact that *the start-up bank loan ... has to be serviced* (lines 12–13), but does not say that service sector businesses have problems getting big enough bank loans.
C: The text says that manufacturers have to find more start-up capital (lines 16–17), but does not say that service businesses have used up most of their capital to set up the business.

15 **C**: *can produce stock ... production process* (lines 39–42)
A: It is true that manufacturers make a bigger initial investment (lines 16–17), but the text does not say that they subsequently need less cash than service businesses.
B: They will only invest if they are fairly sure there is already a market for their product (lines 17–19), but this does not help them to deal better with variations in demand.
D: This may be true, but the text only makes reference to the way service businesses may incur promotional costs *like price cuts or free samples* (lines 14–15).

16 **B**: *service providers have to respond instantly to changes in customer demand* (lines 48–50)
A: The phrase *market-oriented approach* does not mean promoting a business through advertising, although a business may well do this once it has identified a new market.
C: Cash flow is influenced by seasonal changes (lines 34–36) and, of course, by changes in consumer demand (lines 36–44), but this is not a definition of *market-oriented approach*.
D: Price sensitivity is an important factor in winning and keeping customers (see final paragraph), so it will be an element, but only one of several elements, in a *market-oriented approach*.

17 **C**: *caught with huge stocks of unwanted products* (line 57)
A: We are told that service providers *have to respond instantly to changes in customer demand* (lines 49–50), but nothing about whether manufacturers can respond quickly or not.
B: The text refers to *seasonality* (line 38), but it does not say all businesses are affected by it.
D: Cash flow and keeping to budgets are important issues, but there is nothing to say that they are more serious for manufacturers than for service businesses.

18 **B**: *It's much harder to judge ... refrigerators.* (lines 66–68)
A: This is true (lines 16–17), but the text does not link this to higher profit margins.
C: The text only refers the promotional costs of service businesses (lines 14–15).
D: This may be true, but the text specifies only that the difference between cost and price can be greater for manufactured products.

pp.98–99 READING Part 4

0 A
growth relates to *is increasing* in the previous sentence; *count* and *result* do not fit the meaning of the sentence; *progress* is something positive, but the text is about waste (i.e. something negative)

19 B
driven on makes no sense; the lights *remained/stayed* on because the staff left them *switched* on

20 C
damage a machine; *hurt* or *offend* a person; *spoil* = ruin something, e.g. a meal by overcooking it

21 A
lack of knowledge = not having the knowledge; *need/want* of knowledge are possible, but we no longer use these words in this way; a *gap* = a space or hole

22 D
Failure to do something = not doing it; *neglect* is the result of failing to do something; *prevention* and *loss* do not fit in this context

23 D
one thing *leads* to another; *come, take* and *keep* do not fit in this context

24 B
realize = managers are not aware of the costs; *decide, explain* and *produce* do not fit in this context

25 A
All the words are possible, but only *Conservation* fits the meaning of the text.

26 C
saving the money, i.e. not wasting it; *sparing* it would mean not using it/using very little of it; you *control* the waste, not the $55m; you *remove* the problem, i.e. the waste, not the money

27 C
total, i.e. all the elements of electricity consumption added together; *same* does not fit the meaning, and *all* does not fit grammatically; *whole* emphasises the idea of *all*, not part of something, e.g. *We spent the whole day reorganizing the filing system.*

28 A
estimates = makes an analysis and then predicts what will probably happen; *proposes* = suggests; we *foretell* the future; a government agency would not *guess*, it would analyze something carefully

29 B
expected, i.e. the agency expects consumption to double; they *tell* us that it will double; we *await* the results; they *argue* that, i.e. give reasons why it will double

30 B
a town/city is divided into *districts;* a country into *regions;* a report, etc. can be divided into *sections; environment* does not fit the context

31 D
running we can leave a machine running; air *circulates;* when we say that a machine is *going*, it usually means that it is not working properly, but has not broken down yet; videos, CDs, etc. *play*

32 C
(not) in use is a fixed expression, i.e. when the machine is (not) being used; *in place* = where it should be; people who are *in work* have a job; *in time* means *not too late* or *gradually*

33 D
fully **utilized,** i.e. made maximum use of; pets and minds are *exercised*; to *operate* a machine is to switch it on and use it properly; difficult situations or people are *handled*

p.100 READING Part 5

0 CORRECT

00 THAT
So you use ... means *When this is so/In this situation, you use a ...*
Confusion with *so that*, e.g. *Pin the notice in reception so that everyone will see it.*

34 A
lots of ...
Confusion with *a lot of.*

35 IF
let us **say that your** *company ... has a website*
Read the whole sentence first and you will see that there is no *if*-clause.

36 ARE
you type in
Confusion with *you are typing*, which would not fit here anyway.

37 CORRECT

38 WHICH
search engines should be able to find it
Read the whole sentence first and you will see that there is no *which*-clause.

39 UP
make contact
Confusion with *make up*, e.g. *The petty cash is short. Shall I make up the difference out of my own pocket?*

40 CORRECT

41 AWAY
As far as new customers are concerned, ...
Confusion with *far away*, e.g. *I was too far away from the platform to hear what the speaker was saying.*

42 THE

*not understood, **at least** in the UK*
A fixed expression without *the*. Possible confusion with the expression *at the very least*, e.g. *The least you can do is say you are sorry to him. = At the very least, you should apologize to him.*

43 BY

*Imagine ... and **then leaving** copies sitting in a box.*
Read the whole sentence first and you will see that there is no *by* ... *-ing*-clause.
Confusion with *By leaving them in a box, you make sure that nobody will ever see them.*

44 ALSO

*are **just as inaccessible*** (as brochures left in a box)

45 WHEN

even some website designers do not yet understand
Read the whole sentence first and you will see that there is no *when*-clause.

FURTHER PRACTICE AND GUIDANCE (p.101)

1 1 be in touch
2 correct
3 correct
4 make fun of
5 correct
6 do business with
7 come to terms with
8 move premises
9 take care of
10 pay attention to
11 correct
12 correct

2 1 The firm has had a really bad year, so pay increases are out of THE question.
2 Every day, at least six of our machines are out of order. It isn't good enough!
3 If people want quality, they have to pay for it. The price increases we have introduced may lose a few customers at first, but my guess is that in THE long run we will outperform our competitors.
4 Officially, I am supposed to say that everything is fine, but off THE record, the company is in serious trouble.
5 Everyone has worked really hard, and I want to thank the sales staff in particular for their efforts.
6 There have been a few problems with the start-up, but nothing out of THE ordinary.
7 The premises burnt down so we had to start the business again from scratch.
8 Because of the downturn in business, everyone will be on a three-day week until further notice.
9 Our mission statement is very important: everyone should know it by heart.

10 Your spelling is terrible. You even spell your own name incorrectly! Do you do it on purpose?
11 Take these packages to Deptford, and call in at Head Office on THE way.

p.102 WRITING Part 1

Sample answer

Lynn Carter, a school leaver, will be with us for work experience this summer. I suggest she starts in housekeeping and the restaurant. She can then work in reception to get experience of dealing with customers. Let me know about her progress as I must write a report on her.

[50 words]

The note covers all the points:
• details about the girl: her name and that she is a school leaver coming for work experience
• possible departments: *housekeeping/the restaurant/reception*
• help with final report: *Let me know about her progress as I must write a report on her.*

p.103 WRITING Part 2

Sample answer

Location
Westfield Industrial Estate has two or three units vacant, but they are too small. We might buy and develop the neighbouring field. The owner will discuss.

Communications
The motorway to the east has easy access. The railway runs through the town centre. The goods yard is to the SE, but we ship mainly by road.

Housing
There are many old properties near the centre, most of which are rented. There are always properties on the market, so workers' housing is not a problem. The upmarket housing is expensive and suitable for executives.

Grants
The town is in an Enterprise Zone. We might get a grant if we relocate here. This needs to be investigated further.

Conclusion
Providing we can get the field and a government grant, the town is well suited to our needs.

[135 words]

FURTHER PRACTICE AND GUIDANCE (p.104)

1 1 It might be too small to house the factory.
 2 It could be bought and developed. The owner is willing to sell.
 3 They use the road network rather than the railway.
 4 It's mostly rented. Properties are always coming on the market to rent or buy.
 5 It is an expanding estate of expensive houses, suitable for executives.
 6 Because the town is in a government/EU Enterprise Zone (i.e. a region where the government wants to encourage new industry).

2 1 *some places* is too vague: specify the number of units and say that they are available
 2 Too vague and long. Just say they are not big enough.
 3 More detail needed. Is the field part of the Industrial Estate? Are there units on it already? Who owns it? Is it for sale?
 4 Too vague. Where are the motorway and the railway in relation to the Industrial Estate? What about the goods yard? Is there a problem?
 5 Good. Contains all the necessary information – condition, location, use and availability of the housing.
 6 Not enough information. Where is it? What about prices? Who could live there?
 7 Good, but is there any other information you could add (for example how to apply, size of grant)?
 8 This recommendation lacks focus. You should give a full conclusion: it will be a good place to relocate to if certain conditions are fulfilled (i.e. that there is enough space for the factory, and that the firm can get a grant).

pp.105–106 LISTENING Part 1

Conversation 1

1 *toy* (The man says, 'Oh, we make soft toys. You know, teddy bears and such like.')
2 *machinists* (The man says, 'They don't need qualifications but they need to be excellent machinists.') Don't confuse this with the ability to cut out material which is also mentioned but not required.
3 *night shifts* (The man says, 'Oh, and another important thing is that we must have people who can do a night shift now and again.')
4 *six* (The woman says, 'So, six.' The man asks to interview eight or nine people but the woman at the agency says they will screen out anyone unsuitable.)

Conversation 2

5 *Friday* (The woman says, 'I've got some visitors coming for a meeting on Friday.' Monday is also mentioned as the day she was given confirmation that they were coming.)
6 *sandwiches* (The catering manager says, 'I can do a selection of sandwiches and a creamy dessert.' They go on to talk about hot food but then decide to stick with the sandwiches.)
7 *Seminar Room* (The catering manager suggests bringing the food to the meeting room, 'Or you could have it brought up to you. Where's the meeting?' and the woman replies, 'In the Seminar Room on the fourth floor.')
8 *Sales* (The catering manager thinks she works in Marketing but the woman says, 'Actually, I work in Sales now.')

Conversation 3

9 *9 a.m./09.00* (The man says, 'Engel and Volker? Yes, they're coming at nine.' and goes on to mention they have another meeting at eleven.)
10 *South Africa* (The man says, 'After that you've got the group from South Africa coming on Tuesday evening.')
11 *report* (The woman says, 'Then I'm not here on Wednesday. I need the peace and quiet of home to complete that report.')
12 *merger proposal* (The man says, 'It's not about the AGM, though. He wants to discuss the merger proposal.')

p.107 LISTENING Part 2

Section 1

13 **B** (The clues are: 'a creative service plus some fairly sophisticated technical skills.' Mention is also made of using it to promote a company, new technology, a channel of communication.)
14 **G** (The clues are: 'It doesn't help when half the world suddenly becomes dangerous to visit, either.' Two weeks' holiday in Spain is also mentioned.)
15 **C** (The clues are: 'paying out the premiums' and calling for help when they 'lose their valuables on holiday or their mobile phone gets stolen'.)
16 **A** (The clues are: lots of examples of what they do including, 'We will place up to six of our staff in your company and identify major issues and problems.')
17 **H** (The clues are: 'technology systems' and 'We have been able to set up a totally secure system for one large international company that allows its staff to access their computer system from 40 major countries worldwide.')

Section 2

18 D (The clues are: 'the cost of weekend working is so great and simply by doing a few extra hours at the normal time rate during the week instead we can avoid paying double time on a Saturday afternoon and even more for a Sunday.')

19 F (The clues are: 'The last thing you want a potential new employer to think is that you're unreliable' and 'Imagine what you want to say.')

20 C (The clues are: 'it allows individuals to come up with a personal training programme for themselves' and 'It forces people to confront their own weaknesses as well as their strengths'.)

21 B (The clues are: 'most of the work stations in this office are really badly designed' and 'they aren't designed to support all the electronic gadgets we need'.)

22 G (The clues are: 'but you'd be surprised how often you can't find anyone to cover the phones at lunch time because they've all decided to take a long lunch break' and 'but that gets much more difficult at holiday times or when there's a deadline to meet.')

pp.108–109 LISTENING Part 3

23 A: *Two years ago* **when my business was only a few months old** *I decided it needed to expand rapidly.*
B: He decided to expand his business two years ago.
C: He decided to go into business six years ago.

24 B: *These groups of wealthy individuals get a stake in a new company in return for an unsecured cash injection. I also hadn't much experience in management and I wanted to be able to benefit from their experience …*
A: His family hadn't heard of Business Angels and thought he should go to someone with a good reputation.
C: His family and friends had helped him in the past.

25 B: *As part of my course, I had heard about Business Angels …*
A: He didn't think it was any good to ask his bank manager for that sort of money.
C: His family hadn't heard of the scheme before.

26 C: *I had to keep the business running while putting a great deal of energy into preparing the all-important business plan.* **It's the quality of this which really decides whether you get the funds or not.**
A: He was asked questions when he went to the open day.
B: He says that getting investment from Business Angels is very competitive.

27 A: *It was more than I could have hoped for.*
B: This was just one of the things he was able to do.
C: It was more than he needed.

28 C: *I'm planning a new range of products based on the results of the advertising campaign I initiated as soon as I received the cash.*
A: He hopes to open another shop next year.
B: He hopes to do this in the future (see C above).

29 A: *Of course they are going to have a share of the equity when the time comes but that is what you have to accept as part of the deal.*
B: He says they have very little influence over the business.
C: They will have a proportion of the profits, but they will do this by having shares (equity) in the company.

30 A: *I think it's got a lot to do with the risk of investing in the stock market at the moment.*
B: He says he may not make a lot of money.
C: They have little influence over the business.

FURTHER PRACTICE AND GUIDANCE (pp.110–111)

1 1 a product
   2 a skill
   3 a shift
   4 a number
   5 a day of the week
   6 a type of food
   7 a room
   8 a department
   9 a time
   10 a country
   11 an activity
   12 a topic

3 13 A false, B true
   14 A true, B false
   15 A true, B false
   16 A false, B true
   17 A true, B false

4 1B 2F 3C 4G 5D

5 1 owner
   2 friends, family
   3 bank manager
   4 wealthy
   5 stake

SPEAKING

FURTHER PRACTICE AND GUIDANCE (pp.115–116)

1 1G 2I 3B 4C 5D 6H 7E 8F 9A

2 1b 2d 3e 4a 5c

LISTENING SCRIPTS

TEST ONE

Part 1, Conversation 1

Woman: Hello. Is that David Jones?
Man: Yes, speaking.
Woman: I'm Linda Wade and I'm calling about the course next week.
5 **Man:** Which course is that?
Woman: The one for Health and Safety.
Man: Right. I'll have to find the training forms. Have you got the letter?
Woman: Yes, I see. It's on the eighth, no, the tenth.
10 **Man:** .... of April. Is there a reference number ... next to the name of the course?
Woman: Oh, you mean D-J-slash-26-slash-0-4-0-3?
Man: Ah, no. That's my reference. It should begin with A1.
15 **Woman:** Silly me, yes. It's A109R.
Man: Right. I've got the course details here. It's with John Briggs.
Woman: Mr Biggs? [*laughs*] You say we have to wear comfortable clothes, a track-suit or
20 something. Well, I haven't got one.
Man: It's Briggs, actually. He's the course leader for the day. Well, anything that you don't mind lying on the floor with and getting a bit dusty.
25 **Woman:** Why do I have to do that?
Man: Well, as I explain in the course notes, you may have to practice helping an injured person. Also, you'll be trying out the fire-extinguishers and other safety equipment.
30 **Woman:** Crikey! Is there going to be a fire?
Man: No, nothing like that.
Woman: OK then, final question. Where is it?
Man: Room 16. It's a seminar room in the West Building.
35 **Woman:** Next to the canteen?
Man: Yes, that's right.
Woman: OK, thanks.
Man: Bye.

Part 1, Conversation 2

Man 1: This is Paul Ryman's voicemail. I am away from my desk at the moment. Please leave a message and I will get back to you as soon as possible.
5 **Man 2:** Hello there. It's Mark Nolan here, conference manager for Winston House. I'm phoning about the arrangements for the workshops at the weekend. As you know, we have reserved three rooms for you. You
10 were going to let me have some numbers so that I can decide which room to give you for the plenary sessions. If it's more than

thirty, I can offer you the Main Hall but, as I said, that will hold up to a hundred so perhaps it might be too large? There is the 15 Garden Room which might be better. It's in our extension and will take up to fifty. Very nice, bright room. Then the two smaller rooms for up to twenty each. Well, they are on the second floor of the main hotel and I 20 just want to check that that's OK with you. I think you said you needed wheelchair access and I want to reassure you that there is a lift. Perhaps you can get back to me on that as well? Oh, and finally you mentioned 25 car parking. There is a big function on the same weekend so what we're thinking of doing is reserving places for your delegates. Obviously I need to know how many will be coming by car. So, that's about it. Mark 30 Nolan from Winston House on extension 457. I look forward to hearing from you. Thanks.

Part 1, Conversation 3

Man: It's Peter Dowling. I've just received a wrong invoice.
Woman: Right, Mr Dowling. If the order is wrong, I need to take some details from you.
Man: Fine.
5 **Woman:** Could you confirm your customer number?
Man: It's 1005016900.
Woman: And is that order number W36936QCPF?
Man: Almost. The last letter isn't F, it's J.
Woman: That may be why there's a problem. What 10 products did you order?
Man: Two things. A desk and that seems to be what it says here and then ...
Woman: A Parnell Corner Desk at £394?
Man: That's right. But then it says here that I 15 ordered a chair. It should be a filing cabinet!
Woman: So I'll amend this order. Just for your reference the product code is 6693. And the cost is £189. That gives us, with postage and packing, the sum of £596.90. 20
Man: Well no, actually. I was told that orders over £500 are free.
Woman: Sorry, sir. You are quite right. So that brings the total to £583. It will be with you within the next ten days. 25
Man: Thanks. I'm glad that's sorted out. Bye.

Part 2, Section 1

Thirteen I've been working here for nearly five years and I still enjoy meeting the guests and helping them with their problems. Most people are really nice and even those who aren't, well, there's usually a reason. You know, their room is dirty or the TV doesn't work or they've lost their key.

Fourteen Most of the events I'm in charge of are fairly large. Last week I had to find somewhere big enough to take over two thousand delegates in one room. And of course the more people you have to deal with the more things that can go wrong. On one occasion I had five hundred people due to arrive at this hotel in Brighton and the catering staff walked out. Yes, they simply disappeared! Nightmare! I ended up having to employ students from the local college. Fortunately, most of them were on a catering course so they knew how to cook.

Fifteen I took over from a long line of men. In fact I'm the first woman in this position since Sheila Granger, who started the company twenty years ago. My style is very different, though. I believe that a company will be successful if you have three things ... a happy workforce, a good product and an effective marketing strategy. My job is to ensure that my managers can be relied on to produce all three. If they do, I leave them in peace. If they don't, then they're out ... pronto!

Sixteen When I first started in this business, a lot of people were technophobes. I mean they were frightened of computers! They were always ringing me up and saying they had lost all their stuff because they had pressed a key by mistake or they didn't understand why they couldn't get into their emails. Nowadays I think most staff are happy with the basics and I get more interesting things to sort out.

Seventeen I suppose you have to be fairly good at numbers but, to be honest, the computer does most of the calculations these days. My job is more to oversee things and make sure that the books balance at the end of the day. It's not difficult but I have to be organized and make sure that everything is recorded. I suppose I've got that sort of mind. Funnily enough I'm not so good with my own money. I'm often overdrawn by the end of the month!

Part 2, Section 2

Eighteen The only trouble with Bill is that he just doesn't look like a manager. It's difficult to take someone seriously when their shirt's hanging out and their tie's at an angle. His desk is even worse! There are papers all over the place and files on the floor. Last week I swear there were more files on the floor than on his bookcase. It looked terrible in there! Funny thing is that he always knows where everything is and he's a good manager.

Nineteen What I find difficult is that he doesn't give us a chance to do the job before he's having a go. He seems to think we don't know anything and have to be told what to do all the time. The truth is we've been here a lot longer and I think he probably just needs to tell us he's in charge. I don't think it works, though. I know I react badly when someone tells me to do what I'm already doing.

Twenty She's great to have in the office. Always laughing and joking. But what irritates me is that she doesn't do anything and she gets away with it. Last week she sat at her desk painting her nails for at least half an hour. That's probably OK now and again but she makes a habit of it. The worst thing is that she sits around chatting when we are desperately trying to meet deadlines and stopping us from working. I like her, all the same though.

Twenty-one He's always banging on about what problems the company is having and then forgets to explain how the staff can help to improve things. He's good at saying what's wrong but not how we can help to put it right. I think he expects us to all jump to attention if he says something but the truth is it's a lot more complicated than that. We're people, not machines. I guess his real problem is that he doesn't know how to talk to the staff.

Twenty-two Harry? Oh, he'll be about twenty minutes late as usual. I don't know what it is about him but he can't get to a meeting on time. Apparently his PA has started telling him meetings start half an hour earlier than they really do so that he gets there on time. Doesn't seem to have worked today, however! Someone told me that he's just the same at home. He drives his family mad when they all want to catch a plane or something. You can imagine!

Part 3

Woman: My feeling, Alain, is that we can't blame the workforce for our problems. I accept that there has been dissatisfaction with bonus payments and that productivity has fallen but that's not enough to explain the downturn in profits. I believe the marketing department has got to consider a more dynamic approach. After all ...

Man: Come on, Lisa. It's impossible to keep all the staff happy all of the time. And you can't say that the marketing people don't have good ideas sometimes. I think we

15 have to look elsewhere. I actually believe that it's cheap imports that are mostly to blame. We should be looking at how some of these countries can make the same product and charge 50% less.

Woman: Well, from what I understand, they work 20 longer hours, and they don't pay anything like the overtime rates we do.

Man: Not a lot we can do about that. The Union would be totally against reducing overtime rates.

25 **Woman:** I agree, but if we are going to increase profits we have to look at a reduction in staff numbers in certain areas, perhaps with more attractive bonus payments for increased productivity?

Man: It's worth looking at. What do you think we 30 should do next, have a quiet word with the CE?

Woman: I'd rather run it past the Board on Tuesday. After all, the Chief Executive is going to be there.

35 **Man:** I agree, let's talk to them all about it then.

Woman: OK. So what should we put into the strategic plan, then? I've been working on the economic forecast for the next five years but that's not going to be ready by Tuesday.

40 **Man:** Never mind. It's not essential. I think the most important thing is to outline what we think the company should look like, how we plan to cut down on staff, and say that based on our research so far ...

45 **Woman:** We haven't done any!

Man: I know but that's not the point. All they need to think about at this moment is that they have to accept that a complete reorganization is necessary.

50 **Woman:** I suppose so. I don't think we are going to get a good response from the staff when they hear about job losses. You can't really expect them to see that the company's situation is serious.

55 **Man:** No. But with a bit of persuading I think most of them will agree to the new conditions. It's either agree or go, really. End of story.

Woman: You're a hard man, Alain. I expect you 60 would be quite happy for me to be made redundant.

Man: To be honest, if the right package came along I'd be a fool not to accept, but you ... I think you could do well out of this.

65 **Woman:** What do you mean? Ask for a big pay rise for having such a wonderful idea?

Man: Not exactly, but perhaps you could sort of suggest how useful you could be in seeing it all through ... I can see you as the director 70 of operations!

Woman: I don't think you're being serious, Alain. This is much too risky to laugh about. What I can't understand is how, after all this, you'd be prepared to leave. I thought you were happy here.

75 **Man:** I am, I am. Come on you know I won't go yet. Trust me!

Woman: You'd better not. Anyway, what do we do next? Get something down on paper and give the CE a copy?

80 **Man:** No way! Let's go and have a drink before we go home. We need to do some more thinking.

Woman: OK. As long as we have something more concrete before the end of the week.

85 **Man:** Stop worrying, Lisa. Let's go!

TEST TWO

Part 1, Conversation 1

Woman: Hello, is that Alpha Productions Ltd?
Man: Yes, it is. Good morning. Can I help you?
Woman: I was wanting to speak to Henry Lee.
Man: Henry? Sorry, he's out all day, I'm afraid.
5 Can I take a message?
Woman: Yes, please. I'm Maria Greenhalgh. It's about our meeting on Thursday. I'm going to have to postpone it.
Man: Right. You're Maria ...?
10 **Woman:** Greenhalgh, G-R-E-E-N-H-A-L-G-H.
Man: Is that the meeting at two thirty in the afternoon at the operations building?
Woman: I think it's at four. To discuss the plans for the new factory.
15 **Man:** I see, yes, of course. You're the architect?
Woman: Yes. I work for Schneiders. What I was wondering is can Mr Lee make it the following Tuesday morning at eleven?
Man: I'll just check. Possible, but Wednesday at
20 eleven is better. He has a short meeting at nine but he should be free the rest of the day.
Woman: OK then. I'll confirm in writing. Could you ask him to bring the stuff on Health and
25 Safety he's had approved? I've got several suggestions to make about the designs for the fire escapes.
Man: Sure. I'll make a note.
Woman: Thanks very much.
30 **Man:** Not at all. Bye.
Woman: Bye.

Part 1, Conversation 2

Man: Have you seen this complaint from Freeman's, Laura? It's that last IT delivery we sent out to them.
Woman: Oh no, not again. Was it damaged? Last
5 time two monitors were broken.
Man: No. It seems that they're missing at least three PCs and they only received four printers.
Woman: How many should they have had?
10 **Man:** They say six.
Woman: I bet they're furious, aren't they?
Man: Yes. It doesn't stop there, though. Apparently we rang them to say the delivery was delayed until next week but it
15 got there yesterday after all and there weren't enough people on duty to unload.
Woman: What a mess. Are they asking for compensation?
Man: Yes. They want us to make them an offer to
20 cover the extra staff they had to bring in.
Woman: Let's have a look at the message. Oh dear. Yes, they are cross. I think we're going to have to consider it.

Part 1, Conversation 3

Woman: Oh, hello, yes. I'm enquiring about that job you've advertised in today's paper. It's for a data input clerk in the Marketing Division ... no, sorry, the Sales Division, isn't it? Yes.
5 Well, what I want to know is if you do flexitime. I mean, I see it's for 30 hours a week and I want to know if you allow say an early start at eight and leaving by two. I could leave at three but two would be
10 better. Anyway the other thing is the pay. It says 'according to experience'. I've done this before so would I get the £9.40 an hour? The lower rate, that's £6.40, wouldn't really be enough. Anyway, if you could get back to me. My name's Sophie Clarkson and I'm
15 on 020834588. I'll be here this afternoon until about six, otherwise I'll ring again in the morning, if that's OK. Thanks. Bye.

Part 2, Section 1

Thirteen It's a good idea if you can find out in advance what their interests are. You might think an expensive evening out sounds wonderful, but perhaps he or she may be tired and not feel like getting dressed up and going somewhere posh! They might just prefer a meal in a quiet restaurant followed by an early night. After all they could have been travelling for hours!

Fourteen It's almost always advisable to wear a suit unless you are absolutely sure that the dress code is different. It goes without saying that you shouldn't be late so allow yourself plenty of time to get there and have a few minutes to relax and check yourself in a mirror. When you shake hands, look them in the eye and smile. Try and answer the questions without repeating yourself too much and, above all, try to speak slowly. When you're nervous, you tend to speak too quickly.

Fifteen Well, the first thing is to make sure you've got all the documents you need. If possible, you'll have already let them know that you're calling so that they've had time to prepare. Once you get through, remember the other person may not understand you easily so try to speak slowly and clearly. As they can't see your reactions, always confirm that they've understood each point that's been made. And, don't pretend you've understood them if you haven't.

Sixteen The first thing to think about is what the primary purpose is. By that I mean, who is it for, why do they want it and what are they going to use it for. It's probably going to be sensible to think about the main body of it and leave the introduction until later. Finally check the grammar, spelling and write the recommendations. When it's complete, you could try reading it aloud to someone who might give you some constructive comments on it.

Seventeen It's not a good idea to use complete sentences. Remember to use abbreviations whenever you can but not so many that you can't understand them later. Try putting in words like *because, therefore, but* or *as* as they can show how your ideas are related. Use lots of space so you can expand them later if you need to. Remember to use the dash as it's a very useful punctuation mark.

Part 2, Section 2

Eighteen They're not a bad bunch of people. On the contrary, I think we've got some really hard working and committed staff. No, the trouble is that they are mostly new to their jobs and they are taking a lot longer to understand what they are supposed to be doing. Longer than I expected, I'm afraid. I think I assumed they'd be very quickly up to speed, but at this rate I'm seriously thinking about putting on some training programmes and workshops. What do you think?

Nineteen I think he's done an excellent job. In fact, that's going to be part of the problem. I mean it's going to be very difficult to replace him. I know we'll find people eager to take on the role but not someone who can give what he gave. I don't think he wants to go, actually, but he has no choice. He's been in the job for six years and the rules say he has to go. Pity.

Twenty There's not a lot we can do about it. It's the same story all over the world at the moment. People simply aren't choosing to invest their money in the market. I know it's done particularly badly over the last few months but as a company we are sound and the sales figures are up again, and we are looking for new suppliers. We should be proud of what we've achieved. The market will recover in the end.

Twenty-one Yes, I agree that this is an issue we have to tackle immediately. If we don't produce a good and reliable product, we might as well close the business. Some of the staff are saying it's the result of bad management but my view is that we need to investigate the quality of our suppliers. I've heard that there is a serious problem with the standard of some of the basic ingredients.

Twenty-two I've had a word with the senior managers about it. They seem to think that the main issue is low salaries. In my opinion it's more to do with working conditions here. The new shift arrangements are making life difficult for many people. After all, the majority of the workforce is women with families. No wonder they can't make those early starts and late evenings.

Part 3

Man: Good morning from *Business Matters*. I'm Ed Stanton and we'll be talking today about how IT and in particular the Internet can help your business. I have Christine Stainsbury in the studio who runs her own herb and spice business from home and who has recently 'gone live' on the web and now markets her products to customers all over the world. Christine, thank you for joining us. What's been good about the web for you? [10]

Woman: Good morning, Ed. Yes, I'm absolutely delighted with my website. I was told that it would save me thousands on brochures and postage, etc. and it may well do that in [15] the future but what I'm really pleased about is how I'm getting to know my customers better.

Man: Why is that so important?

Woman: It means I can start to tailor my products to [20] what they really want. So I sell more.

Man: I see. So what's changed?

Woman: Well, for example, I use email rather than the post. It's easier and simpler for the customer and I just build any marketing [25] questions I have into the order form. I'm beginning to establish a good working relationship with some of my regular customers.

Man: So what do you need to do before you [30] create a website? I suppose you need to sell the stuff over the web, don't you?

Woman: Well, yes. The first decision you must take is whether to sell over the Internet or not. I do, but you don't have to. Then there are [35] other decisions to make later on in the design process such as whether customers will be able to access information about how their order is progressing.

Man: What next? [40]

Woman: Well, if you don't feel you have enough specialist knowledge then consider bringing in a website designer but, more importantly for everyone, make sure you give sufficient resources to the process. [45] Even if you do delegate most of the design work, you may want to add new material from time to time.

Man: And then you have to get people to visit your site? [50]

Woman: Indeed. You can do the usual things such as

put your web address on your business stationery but I've found the surest way to get more hits – that's people visiting your site – is to get your name listed on other sites.

Man: Have things changed for you since 'going virtual'?

Woman: Since I had the website? Completely! I knew that I should be able to introduce new products more quickly and I am just starting to see it happen. I always felt at home with the technology so I have decided to focus on the Internet side of things completely. In fact, I closed my shop down last week and just work from my own office at home.

Man: Right! Do you think most people could do what you have done? Don't they need good IT skills?

Woman: No, not really. But I was surprised at how much time it took in the beginning. If I were to do it all again, I'd employ someone to add new material and so on.

Man: Do you answer all the emails?

Woman: Of course, 100% of them!

Man: And has the business grown significantly?

Woman: It was growing on average at 13% a year. Since I've had the website, it's more like 30%. I hope to increase it by another 10% next year.

Man: Sounds fantastic. What's next on your agenda?

Woman: Well, I'm not going to start another business. I'm not ready for that yet, but now that I've got broadband my costs have reduced so I'm considering taking on staff to run the business while I take a break.

Man: Broadband?

Woman: Yes, it's the latest super-fast way to connect to the Internet. It's faster and cheaper.

Man: So you will have some time to do ... what exactly?

Woman: Well, there's lots to consider. I need some quality thinking time.

Man: Then I'll watch this space!

TEST THREE

Part 1, Conversation 1

Man: It's Mike Ponti from Jarrold's speaking. That's J-A DOUBLE R-O-L-D apostrophe S. This is a message for Katy in Despatch. Katy, I ordered some stationery last week, sorry, I mean catering supplies. Mostly coffee and tea refills for the machines but there's some other stuff as well. They were due to be delivered tomorrow, that's Wednesday. Unfortunately we're closed that day and I was wondering if you could give me another delivery date? After the weekend is best for us, but not Monday if that's possible. It's quite urgent as we've run out of some things already. The order code is, let me see, 456Y – no, that's one of the product codes. It's JR0023. That's right. Also, could you let me know if your new catalogue is out? I'd like a copy, please, if it is. I expect it has the new price-list in it, hasn't it? Could you include it with the order? Great. Thanks.

Part 1, Conversation 2

Man: Training department, Matthew speaking.
Woman: Hello. It's Louise Geller here. Can I speak to Mark, please? He deals with workshops and things, doesn't he?
Man: Yes, that's right. Which department do you work for?
Woman: I'm in Marketing ... sorry, no. We call ourselves the Publicity Department now!
Man: Right. And you want to find out about the new training programme we're putting on? Shall I get Mark to call you back? He's just out of the office at the moment.
Woman: Yes, please. But what I actually want to discuss with him is the possibility of going on a management course. I just got the details today.
Man: Oh, I see.
Woman: Well, I don't know how much is left in the training budget for our department. It seems quite expensive but it's just what I'm looking for.
Man: Right.
Woman: The thing is I'm heading up our West London branch in three months' time. This course would be a real boost for me.
Man: Well, leave it with me and I'll get Mark to call you when he comes back.
Woman: That would be good. Thanks.
Man: OK, then. Bye.
Woman: Bye.

Part 1, Conversation 3

Woman: ABC Car Hire, Mandy speaking.
Man: Hello, there. Gerben Stoller speaking. I'm phoning on behalf of my company, Easy Finance Ltd.
Woman: Good afternoon. How can I help?
Man: I believe you hire cars at competitive prices as long as we set up an account with you.
Woman: You mean the Company Car scheme? It lets you have up to six cars on permanent loan for a minimum of six months. Then there's our Premium Rate scheme where you have an account with us and we let you have cars at a special rate, as long as you hire a minimum of ten cars over a three-month period.
Man: It's the one you mentioned first with the permanent loan arrangement I'm interested in. Can you do us a special deal?
Woman: I think it might be quite a good idea if you came in and talked to the manager.
Man: Yes, I could do that. In fact I'm coming your way tomorrow afternoon – or else sometime next week?
Woman: Let me see. Yes, Mr Parsons will be here tomorrow but he's on holiday all of next week.
Man: Fine. I'll see him then.
Woman: Thank you, sir. Goodbye.
Man: Goodbye.

Part 2, Section 1

Thirteen Hello. It's Frank Mortimer speaking, from Marshall's. It's about our meeting tomorrow at eleven. I can't make it. You remember that big order I told you about? Well, it's due tomorrow so I have to stay here and keep an eye on everything. Apparently the boss doesn't trust the warehouse staff to cope even though they've got written instructions about where to put everything! Could you give me a ring and see if we can do something next week instead? Thanks. Bye.

Fourteen Hi there. It's Judy. Just wanted to explain why I had to leave early yesterday. It was an excellent presentation and I was really enjoying it. Unfortunately my secretary got hold of me and said I'd been called in by the boss. I had already cancelled a meeting with him yesterday so this time I felt I had to go. All he wanted to do was give me a list of things to do before the inspectors arrive. Boring! Anyway, hope you understand.

Fifteen Hi there. It's Rob Brightwell from Newmark Landscape Builders. I just wanted to change something on the list I left with you. I thought about what you said and I think you're right about measuring up the whole area. I do need more paving slabs. I calculated the area incorrectly. So what I'm going to need is another 24 slabs, please. Doesn't matter if they're a slightly different colour. I promise I won't complain!

Sixteen Yes, it's John Ridgewell speaking. I'm calling about a letter I received from a Miss Sally Sayers. She says she has had to return one of my cheques because I had 'insufficient funds' to cover it. She must know my salary was due to be paid in and there's plenty of money in my account to cover it now. This has caused me a lot of embarrassment, I can tell you. The company has cancelled the car I ordered and obviously thinks I'm not credit worthy. Could she call me back as soon as possible? I'm on 01278 456891 and it's John Ridgewell.

Seventeen Hi there. You asked me to tell you about our complaints system. You should have a copy of this somewhere but it's really very simple. What we do is send the customer a copy of our complaints procedure with a covering letter acknowledging their letter and saying the matter is being looked in to. Next, we get hold of the people who we think are involved and get as much information from them about the situation as possible. We have to keep a record of everything we do and who we've spoken to and so on. That's important, I think. Then we don't contact the customer again until we are sure we have all the facts. That's basically it, really.

Part 2, Section 2

Eighteen I'm a bit nervous, to be honest. This will be the first time I've talked to her about what I think the senior staff, including myself, need to develop our skills and so on. I'm not talking about the routine workshops we all have to do, you know, how to handle medical emergencies or how to manage your time better. No, I want some good advice on what sort of courses are available on 'managing risk ' or 'strategic thinking'. After all, we expect our staff to represent the firm overseas and deal with important foreign delegations. Quite high level stuff, really.

Nineteen He's coming this morning, I think. Apparently when we were moving the files from the cabinet into our new room one of the secretaries caught her finger under one of the drawers. She made an awful fuss and she said she might sue the company! It now turns out that she shouldn't have been helping to move the stuff. That's the job of the removals men and we are supposed to sit here and tell them what to do but not touch anything! So this chap is coming to see me and explain all this. I expect I'll find out I'm doing other things I shouldn't be doing according to the regulations so it could be quite useful.

Twenty Did you know that we're getting a visitor today? Yes, it's a François Germain from Paris and it looks like he's interested in the new range that's coming out in the spring. It could be good news for the company as, if he likes the stuff, we could be seeing a very large order. So, anyway, I've got someone from the Research Department to come and do the technical bits and I'm going to give a general presentation. Wish me luck!

Twenty-one I'm going to need copies of everyone's contract for her to have a look at and also any other relevant documents. It's going to be quite an important meeting because until management know where they stand, legally I mean, we can't even think about reducing the workforce. It's all very well those management consultants telling us to reduce staffing levels. Actually doing it without breaking the law requires great care. We are going to have to listen to her advice very carefully!

Twenty-two He's coming around ten, I believe, so we must let security know. He told me on the phone yesterday that there's been a good response to the advert we put in the national press last week. Apparently some of the applicants look really promising. Plenty of management experience, most of them. Anyway, he's had a quick look and wants me to discuss a possible short list with him. After that he'll get everything sorted for the interviews, look up the references and so on. All we have to do is decide who we want to interview and be there on the day.

Part 3

Interviewer: It's a well-known fact that coping with the demands of a full-time job and family life can be tricky at the best of times. However, there are thousands of couples who share the same space 24 hours a day, 365 days a year. Actually, around 70% of businesses in this country are run by families which makes them, statistically speaking, the backbone of the economy. Although productivity does not differ markedly, what is significant is that an average lifespan of nearly 22 years for a

15 family-run business is twice as long as the
average for other companies and with very
low staff turnover of less than 15% over that
period.

Now, Jill and Scott Ridley run the successful
20 Lark Designs Ltd and have been making
high quality garden furniture for over ten
years. Jill, what's it like working 365 days a
year with your husband breathing down
your neck?

Jill: Well, of course he doesn't! One of
25 the warnings that business advisers give is
that working long hours can put too much
pressure on a relationship. However,
provided we share the work equally there
isn't an issue. After all, we work in the same
30 office most of the time and so we know
exactly what needs to be done. We also
encourage each other to take a break now
and then and sometimes this means one of
us taking a whole day off!

Scott: In fact, I once took a whole week off to play
35 some golf in Spain and she never
complained!

Interviewer: Really, Jill!

Jill: Not a word! And then the following month
I took a week off to go shopping in London.

40 **Interviewer:** Then, I'm told that another major area of
tension can be the children.

Jill: One of the decisions we made when we
decided to set up Lark Designs was to share
our childcare duties. Actually, it didn't
45 work out like that. After our second child
was born I worked part-time for a while.
But basically, now, we both work all the
hours under the sun, and we don't have a
problem because we both understand the
50 demands of the business.

Scott: Yes, we manage. Sometimes the children
have to come first and one of us, usually
me, has to work all night to catch up! Not
too often, though.

55 **Interviewer:** Do you never relax?

Jill: Of course, of course. Scott can't play golf
every weekend, although he'd like to and
I've thought about getting a dog so we
could go for a walk in the fresh air
60 sometimes.

Scott: Stop right there ... more work! No, what I
find works best when I'm feeling really
stressed is to put some music on and then I
calm right down.

65 **Interviewer:** So there must be something you
disagree about?

Jill: Not really. I don't look after the technical
side. That's Scott's territory and we have an
accountant to look after the money side of
70 things or that could be a problem.

Scott: We have strong opinions about the best
design for a garden chair or something.

Interviewer: Sort of professional arguments?

Jill: Sometimes we don't see eye-to-eye on
artistic matters. But I think that helps us to   75
produce better products in the long run.

Scott: Yes, and I have far fewer disagreements
with Jill over that sort of thing than I did
with my male colleagues in my last job.

Interviewer: Don't you miss that sort of thing? Going   80
to the pub at lunchtime, having meals out,
paid for by the company?

Jill: No, I don't. I don't miss anything, not even
having a secretary.

Scott: Mmm ... I think on a Monday morning   85
when there's a pile of letters to answer, I
could do with that sort of help!

Interviewer: So what happens next?

Jill: Well, we want to extend our range and that
means more time on the design side of the   90
business.

Scott: We're already increasing our exports and
have had to take on more staff in the factory
and that means we don't have to do many
of the every day things. Which is great   95
because that's what we're both interested
in.

Interviewer: Sounds like a perfect relationship!

Jill: It is!

TEST FOUR

Part 1, Conversation 1

Man: Is that Proplan? It's Harris International here.

Woman: Hello. How can I help you?

5 **Man:** We're looking for some more staff for our production line.

Woman: Could you give me a bit more detail on that, Mr ...?

Man: Morganson. Piet Morganson. Well, we need about two more on each shift. From next
10 week, if possible.

Woman: From the 22nd then. Fine. What is your product?

Man: Oh, we make soft toys. You know, teddy bears and such like.

15 **Woman:** Do you want experienced staff?

Man: Well, yes. There's a lot of sewing involved. They don't need qualifications but they need to be excellent machinists.

Woman: Do they need to cut out patterns from
20 material?

Man: No, that's done already. Oh, and another important thing is that we must have people who can do a night shift now and again.

25 **Woman:** That shouldn't be a problem. Now, how many are we talking about here?

Man: Well, as I said, two more on each shift. There are three shifts at the moment, including the late one.

30 **Woman:** So, ... six.

Man: Well if you can send me eight or nine to interview, I can weed out the ones who aren't up to scratch.

Woman: Don't worry, we'll do that this end. We
35 won't send you anyone who's not up to it. Now if I can take your contact details ...

Part 1, Conversation 2

Woman 1: Hello. Is that catering?

Woman 2: Yes. Julie Gibson speaking.

Woman 1: It's Francesca Wilks here. I've got some
5 visitors coming for a meeting on Friday. Can you do lunch? I know it's not much notice but they only let me know on Monday evening and ...

Woman 2: The 14th? I should think so. I can do a selection of sandwiches and a creamy
10 dessert.

Woman 1: Mmm ... What about hot food?

Woman 2: Something like a seafood starter, followed by lamb or a vegetarian option?

15 **Woman 1:** You know, I think that hot food would be too much for us.

Woman 2: Fine. How many are we talking about?

Woman 1: Twelve.

Woman 2: OK. And do you want the small dining
20 room or the hall over in the new building?

Woman 1: I didn't know that was finished. I'm sure we can all fit in the dining room, can't we?

Woman 2: Or you could have it brought up to you.
25 Where's the meeting?

Woman 1: In the Seminar Room on the fourth floor. Yes, that would save us breaking up the meeting for too long.

Woman 2: Now I need to book it to your division.
30 That's Marketing, isn't it?

Woman 1: Actually, I work in Sales now.

Woman 2: Right, I'll send you an email to confirm.

Woman 1: Thanks, Julie.

Part 1, Conversation 3

Man: Helen, would you like me to go through your appointments for next week?

Woman: Thanks, Sam. That would be good. I know I've got to see the solicitors on Monday. What time's that?
5

Man: Engel and Volker? Yes, they're coming at nine but they said it shouldn't last more than an hour. They have another meeting at eleven so that should hurry them up. After
10 that you've got the group from South Africa coming on Tuesday evening. You're taking them out to dinner and all that's arranged.

Woman: We're going to Gino's, aren't we?

Man: Yes. Sounds Italian but the food's French!

Woman: Fine. Then I'm not here on Wednesday ... I
15 need the peace and quiet of home to complete that report.

Man: Yes, and I won't phone you. Promise!

Woman: Aren't I seeing the Chief Executive sometime this week about the AGM?
20

Man: Yes. You've got a meeting with him at two on Thursday. It's not about the AGM, though. He wants to discuss the merger proposal.

Woman: Then there's Friday!
25

Man: Yes, but everything's ready. You don't need to worry.

Woman: Thanks, Sam. Where would I be without you?

Man: No problem. It's my job.
30

Part 2, Section 1

Thirteen We are a very new business and most of us in this line of work are relatively young. What we are offering is a creative service plus some fairly sophisticated technical skills. Companies are realizing that this method of promoting themselves really works. The majority of people in business today can see how new technology can help their marketing strategy. We can help make it an interesting channel of communication as well as visually attractive.

Fourteen Our industry has suffered a lot lately from the uncertainty in the financial markets and in the world, generally. It doesn't help when half the world suddenly becomes dangerous to visit, either. The thing is, this is a very competitive market and also incredibly price sensitive. The cost of insurance for us is soaring. We find that many people expect that the price of two weeks in sunny Spain should remain the same from year to year.

Fifteen   I suppose some people think of us as an unfortunate necessity. They resent paying out the premiums when everything is going well but then when something dire happens, you know, they lose their valuables on holiday or their mobile phone gets stolen, then they're very pleased to call us up and ask for help. Most companies take it pretty seriously but we still have to find ways of advertising ourselves successfully to the general public.

Sixteen   We have quite a reputation in the field now. We have specialized and what we offer is a tailor-made assessment service. We will place up to six of our staff in your company and identify major issues and problems, evaluate the risk factors, offer practical solutions to them and create an environment in which your staff can manage risk successfully. Sounds complicated but it's actually just common sense. The difference is we can be more objective and daring than staff caught up in their own position in the company.

Seventeen   The thing is, if your technology systems can't keep up with the times then your staff are going to struggle to meet their targets and keep your balance sheet healthy. We offer a service that will make sure systems are properly maintained, fast, and as secure as you need them to be. We have been able to set up a totally secure system for one large international company that allows its staff to access their computer system from 40 major countries worldwide. It won't just save you time; it will save you money as well.

Part 2, Section 2

Eighteen   My suggestion is that you have a meeting with staff to discuss the issue. If you can explain clearly that the company is in financial difficulties then they may be more willing to accept this change. They may not be aware that the cost of weekend working is so great. Simply by doing a few extra hours at the normal time rate during the week instead we can avoid paying double time on a Saturday afternoon and even more for a Sunday. In the long term it may mean the company can stay profitable and that's in everybody's interest, isn't it?

Nineteen   It's a good idea if you can get there early. It gives you time to calm down and check you

look OK! Also, if you give yourself plenty of time then there's less chance of getting held up and being late. The last thing you want a potential new employer to think is that you're unreliable. Then I suppose the next most important thing is to prepare for it. Imagine what you want to say. And whatever you do, don't trip over the carpet or bump into the office furniture as they show you in! Keep calm and smile.

Twenty   One of the important things about this annual review system is that it allows individuals to come up with a personal training programme for themselves. It forces people to confront their own weaknesses as well as their strengths and makes them look at what they can do to improve themselves. I've heard that even the directors are thinking of going on some sort of workshop to improve their presentation skills. Now if they can do it, so can the rest of the staff.

Twenty-one   I think most of the work stations in this office are really badly designed and don't give staff enough space. We should be considering spending some of the budget on having someone produce something special for us. Lots of people say that we've got to update ourselves and replace some of the older work stations because they aren't designed to support all the electronic gadgets we need and still allow us room to sign letters or collate stuff for meetings. What do you think?

Twenty-two   I'm afraid my advice is don't introduce it. It sounds great and of course the staff love it but you'd be surprised how often you can't find anyone to cover the phones at lunch time because they've all decided to take a long lunch break that day. Now I know there are core times when everyone is supposed to be in the office but that gets much more difficult at holiday times or when there's a deadline to meet. I tell you, it's a nightmare!

Part 3

Man: My name's John Hamilton and I run my own company. I'm here to explain to you a bit about Business Angels and what they may be able to do for your company. As you know, it's not easy to persuade someone to   5
give you a million pounds but it's not impossible either. Two years ago when my business was only a few months old I decided it needed to expand rapidly. I had been surviving on cash handouts from   10
friends and family ever since deciding I wanted to go into business six years ago when I was studying financial planning at university. I already understood that it wasn't much good going to see my bank   15

manager for the sort of money I needed and it wasn't possible to ask my family for that sort of money, either.

As part of my course, I had heard about Business Angels and I knew they would be my best bet. These groups of wealthy individuals get a stake in a new company in return for an unsecured cash injection. I also hadn't much experience in management and I wanted to be able to benefit from their experience, which is part of the deal. My family, on the other hand, were rather worried because they hadn't heard of them and thought I should go to someone with a good reputation. It was hard work to reassure them, I can tell you! Competition for investment from Business Angels is very stiff but I gave it all I could. I spent six months preparing the bid which involved doing everything from market surveys to stress tests. I had to keep the business running while putting a great deal of energy into preparing the all-important business plan. It's the quality of this which really decides whether you get the funds or not. Then last year I was invited to an open day where I had to answer questions about my business. That was really stressful! Much more than any exam I had to take at university. But it all paid off. I was offered one point one million pounds worth of funds and two of their investors came onto the board. It was more than I could have hoped for. The cash has allowed me to achieve my goals fast. I've already decided I'm going to open another shop next year and in the meantime I'm planning a new range of products based on the results of the advertising campaign I initiated as soon as I received the cash. It's all very exciting. So I'm very grateful to Business Angels for giving me the chance but I'm also aware that I was in a good position to offer them an investment opportunity even though I am a new company. It didn't matter that I was lacking expertise in some areas. That's been put right by having their two representatives on the board. Of course they are going to have a share of the equity when the time comes but that is what you have to accept as part of the deal.

I think what's interesting in today's financial climate is how willing private investors are to fund small businesses like myself. I think it's got a lot to do with the risk of investing in the stock market at the moment. Despite the fact that they don't really have much control over my business and I may not make them enormous sums of money, I think I'm probably a very sound investment for the future.

CD TRACK LISTING